Edited by Susan C

beyondwords

Translating
the World

Library and Archives Canada Cataloguing in Publication

      Beyond words : translating the world / editor: Susan Ouriou ; authors: Sara Fruner ... [et al.].

Some text in French and Spanish.
ISBN 978-1-894773-38-6

      1. Literature–Translations. 2. Translating and interpreting.
3. Essays. I. Ouriou, Susan II. Fruner, Sara

PN241.B49 2010   418'.04   C2010-902930-5

Book design by Bob Robertson
Copy Editing by Leslie Cameron
Printed and bound in Canada by Hignell Book Printing
Cover artwork by Bob Robertson

The Banff Centre Press gratefully acknowledges the Canada Council for the Arts for its support of of the Banff International Literary Translation Centre program.

Banff Centre Press
Box 1020
Banff, AB
TIL IH5
www.banffcentre.ca/press

Mixed Sources

Product group from well-managed forests,
controlled sources and recycled wood or fiber
www.fsc.org   Cert no. SW-COC-003438
©1996 Forest Stewardship Council

Contents

The World of Translation

Translating Prose

Preface

Translating
the World

Beyond Words: Translating the World

Susan Ouriou

The art of literary translation is a mystery to many. This anthology is an attempt to plumb the mystery for all lovers of literature—readers, writers and translators alike—as twenty-one literary translators take on the challenge of writing about their craft. The anthology is an eclectic collection by translators working from and into many languages; they come from all over the globe, but share at least one experience. They all have been part of The Banff Centre's annual summer residency on the slopes of Sleeping Buffalo Mountain in Banff, Alberta, Canada, a residency that brings translators together from around the world to hone their craft.

Whether or not literary translators write their own fiction, poetry, drama, or non-fiction, their gift with the written word is what allows them to introduce writers from other cultures and languages to new readers. Some of the translators represented here are recognized artists in the fields of fiction and poetry themselves, while others dedicate all their talent to the art of translation. For the past seven years at the annual international residency in Banff, we have had the good fortune of meeting and working with some of the best literary translators and their authors from around the world; they have generously shared their thoughts on art, craft and literature.

A translation imbued with all the meaning, emotion and vigour of the original never comes about through a literal transposing of one language into another, which explains our title *Beyond Words*. Time and again in these essays, we hear of the challenge translators meet in finding that place beyond words they must return to in order to convey the heart and soul of the original text.

I have described the anthology as eclectic. What else could it be with contributors from some nine countries writing here in one of the three official languages of the Banff residency—English, French or Spanish (sometimes even when that language is not their working language)—and translating in many more, working in a variety of genres and coming from many different, at times even divergent, schools of thought: the intuitive, methodical, philosophical and political among others.

What is truly astonishing is the similarity among the pieces, the innovative use of metaphor—translation as a high wire act, a song sung in harmony, a dance of approximation, sub-version, a twin voice, good sabotage, a clearing of mist, an erotic engagement, a spiritualization, a coupling, a denuding—and the passion required to re-create a work as powerful in translation as in the original. The fascination for the reader is in seeing the multiple ways in which the translation experience unfolds.

Although I have arbitrarily divided the anthology into four parts—Translating the World, Translating Poetry, The World of Translation and Translating Prose—there is, in fact, no clearcut division among the four. There could have been many others still to fully reflect the diversity we have seen over the years in Banff—Translating Theatre, Translating Creative Non-Fiction, Translating the Graphic Novel and Translating Song to name but a few. Perhaps these will require a second anthology at some future date.

The translators represented in the section "Translating the World" reflect on translation's culture-carrying role while in"The World of Translation" translators analyze the act of translation itself. In the sections "Translating Poetry" and "Translating Prose," contributors deal more specifically with individual projects. All are involved in the quest described by former BILTC advisor, Sheila Fischman: "I see us as prospectors who seek beyond the gold, searching for what lies behind what lies behind the words."

The last essay in the anthology comes from the one non-translator among the contributors. Every year in Banff, a few of the translators' authors are invited for one of the three weeks to work with their translator/s. The authors are usually from Canada, the USA or Mexico, but past writers have also hailed from Cuba and Korea. The essays in this anthology mention a few of those authors—Lorna Crozier, Dionne Brand, Horacio Castellanos Moya, Claudine Potvin, Jorge Miguel Cocom Pech and Nicolas Dickner—but many more have participated over the years. In the final essay, Quebec author Nicolas Dickner—who was in Banff with his English translator, also from Quebec, Lazer Lederhendler—gives us a sense of his appreciation of the Banff experience as seen through a non-translator's eyes. My hope is that you, as readers, will have an equally stimulating experience in the company of the Banff contributors throughout these pages.

As director of BILTC and a translator myself, I too have formed my own philosophy around this art I love. I liken translation to the act of exploring the country of another writer's making—the country of the spirit, of the soul—then mapping the emotions, the places, the characters, the sights, the sounds, the tastes and the smells that make up that country in my own language, guiding readers along the path from being lost in the original to being found in their own language. I truly have a sense of going into a world without words to create a translation capable of having the same effect—both notional and emotional—on readers: letting go of first one language, then the other, in order to render what lies beyond the words. This is what we do. Both translators and writers play each other's music, engage in the act of translating body and soul, bring to life versions lying dormant, knit each other's stories, map uncharted territory. The country we are all mapping together is the Universal in all its local manifestations and permutations. We go to that place beyond words where images, thoughts and feelings reside, then return to the written page, a place that holds meaning for us all.

The writer, Paul Auster, once said of our profession, "Translators are the shadow heroes of literature, the often forgotten instruments that make it possible for different cultures to talk to one another, who have enabled us to understand that we all, from every part of the world, live in one world." What better time than now to further the telling of stories in this fragile one world that is ours.

I would like to extend my heartfelt thanks to BILTC's first director Linda Gaboriau for the vision and dedication that led to the creation of the Banff International Literary Translation Centre many years ago in partnership with The Banff Centre, the Canadian and US translation associations (LTAC and ALTA) and the Mexican government (FONCA and SRE). I would also like to thank the members of the BILTC trinational advisory council for their invaluable assistance revising my translations for this anthology, Steven Ross Smith, Director of the Banff Centre Press; Mary Jo Anderson, Banff Centre Press Coordinator; Nick Hutcheson, Publishing Workstudy; my husband Joël Ouriou and the funders and advocates who have made possible the incredible BILTC experiment and experience.

Susan Ouriou, Director, BILTC

Translating the World

Translating
the World

Translation or How to Write: What Do You Think?

Sara Fruner

The 2008 Annual Turin International Book Fair has been summarized in a remarkable book entitled *Ci salverà la bellezza (Beauty Will Save Us)*. It is a collection of thirteen lectures that illustrious international writers, thinkers and philosophers gave during the Fair on that year's appointed topic—beauty. The titles of the contributions range from "Justice and Beauty," through "Beauty is Difficult" and "Past Beauty and Contemporary Ugliness," to "Once Upon a Time was Beauty." A unique exception among the lectures is Erri De Luca's piece entitled "Translating to Become a Writer."

I must confess to being intrigued by the presence of an essay on translation in the middle of essays on beauty. The topic stands out while fitting in; it makes sense. We all know that beauty has as much to do with fine arts and philosophy as with language and words. Both paintings and poems strive for the ineffable emotion called beauty.

As soon as I read De Luca's speech, I felt the need to share his thoughts with the community of translators I'd met in Banff in 2006. I remember how we would bump up against translation issues in the most unexpected situations—walking in the woods, staying up late at night, admiring Lake Louise or drinking beer in a pub. "What do you think?" was how it used to start.

This brief essay of mine is a call to my fellow translators from Banff and, more generally, to fellow translators from around the world, to consider how insubstantial a line there is between translators and writers, and how translation is the real culture-carrier.

Erri De Luca is one of the leading voices on today's literary scene in Italy, but he has been many other things as well. A lorry-driver, bricklayer, store-keeper, member of the 1968 political movement Lotta Continua, politically committed journalist, masterful writer, poet and talented translator. Born in Naples, this wanderer at heart—he has lived in Africa and France—has always been fascinated by the holy word, which led him to learn Hebrew and Yiddish on his own, and even to translate a few books of the Bible. In the lecture included in *Ci salverà la bellezza*, De Luca throws

various issues onto the table, beginning with his own personal experience with writing and language. He broaches translation through an intriguing, unconventional "admiration" approach. He writes:

> Sometimes I have been asked, "What do you have to do to learn to write, to become a writer?" My answer is as follows: learn another language, fall in love with a writer, with a poet or a philosopher who writes in another language, and try to translate him/her into your own language. Make an effort to admire and approximate that beloved language in order to bring it into your own, and even adapt it to your size. When you make the effort out of admiration—not envy —you must be free from any comparison relationship with the figure you're interpreting, and with the writing you're translating; you mustn't compete with the writer in your language by mimicking or rivalling him. It has to be an exercise of sheer admiration. Admiration is intransitive. You do not aim at sounding like, and you do not think of sounding like, you just admire, from a distance. If you make the effort of admiration by translating what you admire into your language, then you will master your own language much better. You will be compelled to stretch it, push it to be more specific, shape it in order for it to match the very emotion that pushed you toward the original writing. This is why I consider translation to be the best writing school ever—translation as admiration, not as a gymnastic exercise (87-88, my translation).

What strikes me here is the inquiry into the feeling that moves a translator toward a piece to be translated, and the position a translator should adopt. According to De Luca, admiration and a lack of imitating designs are the ideal axioms both to translate properly and to manipulate one's own language. In other words, by working on texts written by others— working to bring them into a new cultural space—translators unconsciously train their hand and voice in their own languages, and so nurse their own prospective texts. The process is unconscious, hidden and slow, like erosion, or craft work. Through meticulous analytical study of someone else's text and language, translators become acquainted with the mechanisms underpinning language (both source and target languages), and learn to manipulate those mechanisms in order to express their own experience. Thus, translation is exertion, training, perspiration: the ensuing skill—if combined with an inspired soul—is the perfect ground in which a literary work of art can grow.

Another interesting point highlighted by De Luca is the idea that translators do not simply adapt passively to their language; language is not a marble monolith or an unchanging asset before which translators bow their head, resigned. Translators must pick and pull and carve and hone. "Stretch and shape," De Luca rightly says. I say they must be both

blacksmiths and good saboteurs. The expression "good saboteurs" echoes a comment by Jacques Derrida that has accompanied me throughout my career. Derrida often said that, "Translators are rebels against patriotism." By painstakingly toiling within a linguistic system, they succeed in forcing and breaking it, bringing otherness to it. They act as saboteurs to fuel the familiar with the other, the known with the unknown. By choosing innovative, unconventional or unexpected solutions, translators, as much as writers, act as revolutionaries. They rise up, challenge order—as well as the ordinary—and actively perform politics of change.

To go back to De Luca's statement, only by learning someone else's language can we work on our own language and possibly become writers. Even—or especially—if the language in question is dead. This is what De Luca points out in another crucial passage, related to the Esperanto experiment and his decision to learn Yiddish on his own.

> I don't find it strange that the attempt to devise a common language, Esperanto, has been the work of a Jew seeking to compile all existing stocks into one universal language. A universal language does not suit mankind that well. [...] Scattered throughout the world as they are, languages have allowed mankind to take root in the land. You come from a place if you speak the language of that place, not if you're born there. I know this through the experience of our immigration; millions of our people sought to leave, and were compelled to do so. They pulled one language out of their mouth to take a new one in. In this way they could belong, through language, to that place. So the project of one single common language, such as Esperanto, is not useful; it is not within the grasp of our aspirations. Yet it is the symbol of concord, a single language that everyone can speak, the same language spoken by tigers and frogs [...] Yet one common language cannot save mankind from discord (90).

These words simply echo Canadian Poet Laureate Dionne Brand's lines "language/ seemed to split in two, one branch fell silent, the other/ argued hotly for going home" (28), found in her masterly long poem *No Language Is Neutral,* which relates the experience lived by the poem's subject upon leaving home (Trinidad) and immigrating to a new country (Canada). A new language can silence the old language; similarly a single language such as Esperanto runs the risk of hushing the endless nuances provided by different languages in uttering different human experiences. Basically, this is why, as a single all-embracing language, Esperanto failed. Esperanto is doomed to kill cultural specificities—willy-nilly if it aims, as it does, at universal understanding. And, in a sense, it is doomed to kill translation as well. It enacts a sort of flattening linguistic monopoly, despite

resulting intrinsically from a massive translating operation—as a constructed language, it benefits from phonology, grammar, vocabulary and semantics pertaining to the main Indo-European and Romance languages. A flattening linguistic monopoly would gainsay the truth that each language, by recording the history and culture of a people, is the repository of that people's past. Each language is indeed a breathing archive.

Again, Dionne Brand's long poem comes in handy. To describe the oppression that black slaves experienced in the Caribbean, the poet returns to a masterfully evocative poetic synthesis. "No/ language is neutral seared in the spine's unraveling./ Here is history too. [...] Silence done curse god and beauty here,/ people does hear things in this heliconia peace/ a morphology of rolling chain and copper gong/ now shape this twang, falsettos of whip and air/ rudiment this grammar. Take what I tell you. When/ these barracks held slaves between their stone/ halters, talking was left for night and hush was idiom/ and hot core" (20).

So learning a language, and learning to translate that language, is a way of exploring the history of a population—even questioning that history— and enjoying an opportunity to bring it into a completely different geographical, linguistic, and historical context. We need only read what Erri De Luca has to say about his experience with the Yiddish language.

I had never realized that I, as a post-war child, lacked a language. I didn't know that in Europe a language was missing. I discovered that fact in April 1993. To commemorate fifty years of the Warsaw ghetto uprising and destruction, Rome's Jewish Community organized a trip, and I set off with them. [...] I came back from Warsaw determined to learn Yiddish. I ordered an English grammar of the language. We have had to learn other people's languages. Of course, we are a small country. But English is not the only language: English is an unpretentious and effective substitute. Yet its unpretentiousness and effectiveness worked. Thanks to a Yiddish grammar written in English, I was able to learn. [...] I think it is the only thing to do, the only act late-comers can resort to— learn that language, see the lips of the severed language move again. [...] I believe the only thing a late-comer could do was learn Yiddish—prove history wrong, put it on trial, inform it that it had not managed to wipe out everything and sever a language because that language could start up again elsewhere; it could start again, being whispered, read and sung. I don't believe that bodies can be resurrected. I believe that we meet in the time we have been given, then will see each other no more. Yet I believe that languages can be resurrected. Yiddish will be resurrected (90-93).

In addition to its effect on our language, forcing us to develop that special dexterity that writing requires, translation is responsible for moving whole cultures, a fact as true as it is underrated—especially in Italy. That translation has never been afforded the culture-carrier status it deserves is unfortunately an age-old story, translation's auxiliary nature has always been stressed, rather than its role as a cultural vehicle and respected literary discipline. To learn to translate is to guarantee the survival, development and growth of languages. The interaction, but also the friction, that the translation process generates, gives rise to creativity, as well as to continuous linguistic palingenesis or regeneration. Translation, which I consider to be the conversation in which languages engage with each other, is in fact a life insurance policy for language. Without translation, languages and cultures would be ivory towers, bodies disconnected one from the other and headed for autism, sclerosis. Erri De Luca learned Yiddish on his own—an act of admiration linked to ethnic recovery, an actual rescue. I think translation works to accomplish a similar aim. It draws a language/culture (I see "language" as a synonym of "culture") out of isolation by opening it to the world. Translation makes dialogue possible.

My contribution is solely designed to strike up a conversation among translators in love with words and language wherever they live in the world. De Luca's lecture has been a catalyst for this brief meditation, and I invite my fellow translators to pick up and foster the meditation in an ever-growing, never-ending discussion.

The Erotic Place of Translation

Katherine Silver

Literary translation is neither here nor there: between languages, between cultures, neither in full view nor fully invisible. Translators are often described as caught between the extremes of a series of paradoxes that become irreconcilable dilemmas through our work. Translations are *les belles infidèles*—an expression I first heard in translation in Spanish as something like, "Translations are like women, either beautiful or faithful," but never both.

We—women and translators—are said to be true either to the letter— the body—or the spirit. The language we reproduce on the page is judged to be either too fluent, familiar, complacent, or too literal. Framed thus, translating can feel like a high-wire act over a pit of snakes called aesthetic and ethical compromise, textual betrayal, the limitations of language, the failure to find equivalencies. Some claim that nothing that truly matters— mystery, poetry, resonance, the ineffable—can "really" be translated; it can only be re-created in a new language, as if those two activities— translating and re-creating—were not ultimately the same thing. And yet, despite these pitfalls and dangers, we carry on, day in and day out, failing, missing, betraying, mangling, falling short. Losing?

There is no question that the practice of literary translation is a constant reminder of the plurality of meaning, even truth, and of the importance of context for that meaning. Translators must find some kind of satisfaction in relative equivalencies and imperfect solutions, or quit. But my actual experience when I translate is not primarily one of conflict, self-denial, or subordination. There is a "place" I as translator inhabit with increasing comfort and ease, a place that allows me to affirm, always conscious of the paradox, that the untranslatable—the poetry—is the only thing worth translating at all. Not unrelated, my return to translating seven years ago was in large part due to having fallen in love, with a text, that is. What is more poetic, ineffable, mysterious, and resonant than love?

One might ask, as the song does, what's love got to do with it? My own immediate, intimate experience when facing the text I am translating, or that I am reading in order to evaluate if I want to translate it, is one of engagement—with the text, the word, and ultimately, the world. And this engagement, on this most basic level, could be deemed "erotic."

A few comments about the word "engagement." Rather than use the English participial adjective "engaged," we often use the French term. Somehow, the phrase *"littérature engagée"* has a deeper resonance than "engaged literature" does in English; the French clearly refers to a more conscious tradition. In order to define "engaged literature" in English, one can turn to an internal translation and say "committed literature" or even, though much less explicitly in the US context, "politically committed literature."

To further complicate matters, English uses the word "involved" to talk about somebody who is active in politics. The most common translation into Spanish for "engaged" and "politically involved" is *"comprometido,"* or "committed," wherein the "political" is implicit and the involvement is explicit. The place where these meanings overlap in English is when we are talking about a prenuptial arrangement, where commitment, engagement, and involvement become one.

Which brings us headlong into "erotic."

For this we have John Berger, who wrote a book some thirty-odd years ago called *Ways of Seeing*. He is still, with each new book he writes, teaching me new ways of seeing. He's not a translator, nor do I read him in translation. But the power and strength of his spare, luminescent prose must be somehow related to the fact that he is an Englishman living for four decades in a village in rural France. He lives in a translated world, and his prose seems to contain its own translation, where meaning and means coexist in a dynamic post-translated harmony.

In his 1965 book about Picasso, *The Success and Failure of Picasso*, Berger wrote that "part of the force of sex lies in the fact that its subjectivity is mutual." Forty years later, in an essay titled "The Other Side of Desire," Berger says that he prefers the adjective "erotic" to "sexual" because it is less reductionist. Following Berger's example, let us say, "Erotic, but not necessarily sexual."

What do we literary translators actually do? We engage the text, the corporal or incorporated text. Through it, we engage the Other and the Other world out of which that text emerged and of which it is an integral part. We dig into the text; we penetrate its meaning through its means. And moving away from paradigms of domination and submission, which are necessarily genderized, we also bring the text inside us, arguably to a place before language. We allow it to move with the force of its own

mystery back out into the light in new and decorative garments. The urge to translate might be a desire to clear away the mist, pull aside the veil, denude the text. The hook that maintains that desire might be that the more one unveils the more one feels the text—the skin, the sinews. But language is coy, a tease that never shows itself in full frontal display, that like Aphrodite, keeps a garment on and turns slightly away from the observer.

In that same essay, Berger goes on to talk about desire as a "conspiracy of two" (the French pulsates right there beneath the surface of that phrase, and, under that, the Latin—"conspirare": to be in harmony with, to breathe together). It is a conspiracy that offers a reprieve from pain, from the wound that is implicit in existence; a conspiracy that creates a place, a locus, of exemption. Viewed from the outside, this exemption is a parenthesis because it is a disappearance, a shift elsewhere, an entry into a plenitude.

A place that exists outside of place or in the place of all places. This is quite different than being neither here nor there. But it is akin. We all know, however, that no coupling, no matter how ecstatic, is ever completely harmonious. One and the Other, no matter how close they come, each always remains distinct, in part because this discourse, or intercourse, is alive, thus constantly changing. Where would it take us if we imagined the relationship, or interaction, between the translation and the original, the translator and the text, as dynamic, charged, electric, erotic in the sense of vital and giving of life? And then might we see this dynamism, this imperfect harmony, the struggle to become, as lending translation the freedom rather than the onus of placelessness, the privilege of living in the interstice, both temporally and spatially, the elation of engagement and involvement without attachment?

In his essay "Our Feelings Reach Out Beyond Us," Montaigne writes, via his translator, Donald Frame, that "All passions that allow themselves to be savored and digested are only mediocre."

The translator's relationship to the text may be many things—intense, obsessive, impassioned—but it is never mediocre.

The Music of Translation

paulo da costa

Each particular text requires the translator to tune into its needs. The needs are varied and complex in any transposition from one language, one culture to another. Here I will focus on the exploration of a text's specific musical needs. From the poetic to the technical, and to varying degrees, each text will require assorted scales of attention to facilitate the flow of language. To accomplish this, a translator must be an attentive listener and, in addition, competent at hearing the music in the words. What does the text shout, and what does the text murmur? Will the range of notes touch all ears across all cultures? Translation preserves, transforms and invents. Choices are made. The subtle reverberations require ears equal in might to those versed in translating the songs of the trees.

As a writer and poet I depart from the viewpoint whereby superior texts carry an inherent, coherent rhythm and musicality, ingredients that reinforce the particular excellence of their semantics. An effective translator will embrace a parallel, lucid rhythm in the target language. In my translations, I have not needed to sacrifice meaning in a prose text in order to preserve the underlying musicality.

In translating, I first assess the essence of the work to establish if music—the score—lies at the core of the text as in the case of language poetry or rhyme. At times, the primary need of the poem will speak to the obvious choice I must highlight in translation. At other times, when the need for semantic meaning and music are equally married and essential to the experience, such as in a sonnet or other rhyming, I have opted to highlight meaning. In the instance of language poetry, music will take precedence.

I see two distinct levels of music in a text. The most apparent is exemplified by rhyme and might be called the beat of the poem while a secondary one, subtle and conducted by punctuation, I will call a poem's cadence. In the following example, alliteration from sibilant sounds is the essence of this poem.

MUSIC III
    for Adriana

Rita Taborda Duarte
translated by paulo da costa

Simply
    scholar
    from soporiferous sound
    to sonorous silence
Also
    so,
    sharply sage
    is the solar
          clef

MÚSICA III
    À Adriana

Rita Taborda Duarte

Sapientemente
    sempre
    de soporífero som
    a sonoríssimo silêncio.
Assim
    também,
    sustenidament sábia
    é a clave
          solar

In translating, I value the transposition of the breath alongside the semantics of a text, the word, the cadence, the tempo. I see merit in not reshaping the music of an original text to the rhythm of a target language. Instead, I endeavour to remain true to the distinct music and syntax of the original work. I do not shorten the length of the sentences from the original language because English speech favours sentences significantly shorter than the Portuguese, by this I mean, I do not change the punctuation of a text. Either amputation or prosthesis would change the breath of the sentence, the breath of the book and, as a consequence, the musicality of the text. I am a reader who appreciates the strangeness conveyed in the sound and structure of a foreign text. The strangeness that stays true to the spice and flavour I would expect from a distinct view of the world arriving from another language, voice and culture, and to illustrate this I have included a poem from the Portuguese poet Nuno Júdice as well as my translation.

"IMAGEM"

**O homem que falava sozinho na estação central de munique
que língua falava? Que língua falam os que se perdem assim, nos
corredores das estações de comboio, à noite, quando já nenhum
quiosque vende jornais nem cafés? O homem de
munique não me pediu nada, nem tinha ar de
quem precisasse de alguma coisa, isto é, tinha aquele ar**

de quem chegou ao último estado
que é o de quem não precisa nem de si próprio. No entanto,
falou-me: numa língua sem correspondência com linguagem
alguma de entre as possíveis de exprimerem emoção
ou sentimento, limitando-se a uma sequência de sons cuja lógica
a noite contrariava. Perguntar-me-ia se eu compreendia acaso
a sua língua? Ou queria dizer-me o seu nome e de onde vinha
— àquela hora em que não estava nenhum comboio
nem para chegar nem para partir? Se me dissesse isto,
ter-lhe-ia respondido que também eu não esperava ninguém,
nem me despedia de alguém, naquele canto de uma estação
alemã; mas poderia lembrar-lhe que há encontros que só dependem
do acaso, e que não precisam de uma combinação prévia
para se realizarem. — É então que os horóscopos adquirem sentido;
e a própria vida, para além deles, dá um sentido à solidão que empurra
alguém para uma estação deserta, à hora em que já não se compram
jornais nem se tomam cafés, restituindo um resto de alma ao corpo
ausente - o suficiente para que se estabeleça um diálogo, embora
ambos sejamos a sombra do outro. É que, a certas horas da noite,
ninguém pode garantir a sua própria realidade, nem quando outro,
como eu próprio, testemunhou toda a solidão do mundo
arrastada num deambular de frases sem sentido numa estação morta.

"IMAGE"

The man who talked to himself in munich's central station
what language did he speak? What language speak those lost like that, on
platforms of train stations, at night, when no
kiosk sells newspapers or coffee? The munich
man asked me for nothing, he didn't even look
as if he needed anything, meaning, he looked
like someone who had arrived at the last stage
the stage of someone who does not even need himself. Although,
he spoke to me: in a tongue not resembling a language
capable of expressing emotion
or feeling, limited to a sequence of sounds whose logic
the night contradicted. Was he asking me if by any chance I understood
his language? Or did he want to tell me his name and where he was from
—at such an hour when no train was
about to arrive or leave? If he had told me this,
I would have told him that I too was waiting for no one,
nor was I saying goodbye to someone, in that corner of a german
station, though I could remind him that some meetings depend only
on chance, not requiring a previous arrangement
to occur. That is when horoscopes acquire meaning,
and life itself, beyond them, lends meaning to the solitude that pushes

someone toward an empty station, at an hour when newspapers
are not bought or coffee drunk, restoring a touch of soul to the absent
body — enough to establish a dialogue, although
both are each other's shadow. Since, at certain hours of the night,
no one can be certain of one's own reality, not even when another,
like myself, witnessed all the loneliness in the world
dragged through senseless meandering sentences in a dead station.

An important part of what inspires me to bring texts across languages and cultures is a desire to hear the immense diversity of human approaches to perceiving and singing our inner and outer worlds. Crucial to this cultural interchange is my exposure to the manner in which another culture breathes a language, and by extension, the manner in which it embodies the world, welcoming the musicality of another language, that touch of strangeness, the unusual, almost rough friction in my ear. What might sound odd to my ear in translation might be a translator's choice to stay true to the music of the original text, the synergy of unusual meaning and music to deliver the exquisite.

It is common to hear a literary work sentenced negatively with the words, "it sounds like a translation." Implied in the statement is that the work does not sound English, by extension does not sound *right* and meet the expectations of the reader. To insist on a musical translation that appeases the ears of the target tongue might be akin to arguing that we live in the land of rock or blues or jazz and therefore should experience the songs of another culture translated or adapted to the cadence and tempo of a blues or jazz beat, and justifying such a rationale by claiming it is a familiar resonance in our culture and therefore better understood and assimilated. Fado, Chinese opera, kirtan, Mongolian throat singing and soukous might sound strange to many a North American auditory palate, but does that mean we should adapt them to our familiar Western sounds, spanning from jazz to rock, and listen to the words in a Chinese opera coated in the shell of a jazz tempo and fail to experience the breath of the Chinese opera? I would hope not. In the same way, I find it unpalatable to dub a movie into a target language since I lose the authenticity, the uniqueness of the actor's voice in the original language, a sound connected to moving bodies and spirit. When I lose the actor's identity, I lose the sound of the language itself, language expressed in the crystallized uniqueness of that voice. In a similar vein, it is inconceivable to accept a translation that has adapted the meanings and ideas of a work to our own cultural norm in order to make them more palatable to our values, simply because that would be more digestible to me. The intervention may be with the best of intentions, but it still patronizes and controls the change it pretends

to introduce me to. Why then do we accept and even expect works in translation to mimic the flow of English? Yes, in North America we have no time for a rāga, a song that lasts from thirty minutes to hours. Is a five-minute rāga still a rāga?

As a quick aside going from a concept to the concreteness of the body, and for those of us who understand the world best through the tongue and the stomach, I add this analogy. When I want to offer the authenticity of Szechuan cuisine, I need not diminish its fire and richness for it to be better digested by a North American audience accustomed to blander culinary customs. It is my responsibility to meet and experience the Szechuan cuisine as is. Were the cuisine to change itself to please me it would then become something else, perhaps the hyphenated American-Szechuan hot pot or mapo doufu. In my case, I am not interested in receiving a diminished adaptation of the experience of the spices and fire that distinguish such a cuisine.

Change is on the horizon. The once considered lesser children of the English language, the English of the economic or social fringes, such as Cockney, or the colourful language of the racial fringes of the British empire, from Jamaica to India, the speech patterns of these *englishes* are now accepted in English literary works and are reflected with more frequency on the page. These pidgin, creole, Caribbean or First People speakers have infused the conquering language with new rhythms and influences, and as their social and political visibility surfaces, the English literary canons have accommodated and acknowledged their existence, represented the differences and begun to accept their equal value.

My impulse to bring works across cultures reflects an instinct to challenge myself and the reader. I read works in translation because I seek a challenge, an opportunity to be removed from my cultural habituations, patterns invisible and made visible again by a momentary standing-to-the-side. The degree to which a translator wants to challenge the reader to join him or her in a new landscape, a new experience, will likely rest on a mixture of tolerance to the risk of losing a segment of readers unwilling to rise to the challenge and the publishing house's tolerance to financial risk. Most people appear only willing to engage with the world, art and each other while expending the least possible effort on that engagement. A growing number of arts and cultural producers settle for catering to the lowest common denominator. At present, the final translation will likely reflect as its determining factor commercial parameters, even if they are internalized by the translator as the value of accessibility to the reader, to

the market. Providing something readable. Not that the other options would be unreadable. Not that the market might not be hungry for fresh approaches. The market is fed by those who have decided on their behalf what they need, the market has shaped their needs, and that is all that is available. Not unlike cattle in a pen choosing their preferences from the meagre selection placed at their disposal.

The preservation of the accent carried from an original text when it arrives in the target tongue is not only tolerable but perhaps even welcome. We must examine the reason for having favoured a certain standard of sound over another, which was the acceptance of a diminished range of the inherent music and rhythm of speech. I suggest it is not necessary to blend in to be accepted. These immigrant texts do not want to be diluted and disappear into the defined stream of a national or imperial literature; they want to meet the new culture as equals with their uniqueness contributing to the range of human cultural existence. I see no necessity to erase differences and the inherent separateness. What is different is not odd. To judge something odd reflects the position of power and hierarchy imposed by those in a position to judge. I prefer a reverse approach, to say that an accent, a text dressed in another language is accepted because it is unique and authentic to the person carrying it. Why would it be important to disguise the origin of a text or the origin of a person? The accent provides further insight into the relationship or situation when we are able to locate the context of a person we hear, with whom we converse. It facilitates a more complex understanding of the journey across borders, the experience of communication and, ultimately, the experience of meeting the other.

Para qué traducir a la lengua hñähñu

Raymundo Isidro Alavez

Mi interés por traducir al hñähñu, mi lengua materna, es para divulgar lecturas trascendentales, y de esta manera practicar la escritura en hñähñu, puesto que mi lengua ha sido transmitido en forma oral, muy poco en forma escrita. Sólo en fechas muy recientes se ha producido algunos textos de nivel elemental para su aprendizaje. Las traducciones que he emprendido son para el público diverso y vasto de las diferentes regiones en que se habla esta lengua indígena (algunas regiones de Hidalgo, del estado de México, Querétaro, Guanajuato, Veracruz, Puebla, y unas cuantas comunidades de Michoacán y Tlaxcala).

La identidad de la cultura hñähñu se ha erosionado con el transcurrir de los años, debido a que jamás hemos sido educados para poseer una conciencia propia: para destacar nuestra propia historia. De aquí el interés de haber traducido *Visión de los vencidos*, del Dr. Miguel León–Portilla, obra que es considerado un poema épico y que contiene la historia del arrojo de una jerarquía militar conocida como otomí, grupo valeroso durante la conquista española, La palabra otomí nos fue endilgada por la cultura náhuatl, pero los que somos de esa etnia nos llamamos ñähñu y nuestra lengua es el hñähñu.

Los rasgos culturales de cada pueblo se preservan a través de las tradiciones, que con el tiempo van incorporando nuevas prácticas que impone la vida moderna, porque una tradición está en constante renovación. Se van trasformando al igual que la misma sociedad, cumpliendo con ello las leyes de la dialéctica, que nos dicen que nada es perpetuo, todo se modifica, salvo los sucesos sociales y los vestigios de las obras arquitectónicas que aún existen en la memoria colectiva.

En el mundo científico, en la vida cotidiana y en el ámbito laboral, lo que sabe una persona lo ha adquirido de otros hombres. Sólo que para esto se ha diseñado un idioma para captar todo lo que hay en la tierra y describirlo con certidumbre. Con esa prodigiosa capacidad, habilidad y virtud de captar e imaginar los hechos que para él tienen significado, el traductor se desempeña como el intermediario para transmitir esas ideas y darlas a otros lectores para que éstas sean captadas. Por eso, el traductor se vuelve un innovador, porque cambia su vocabulario, construye términos para dar a entender lo que dicen los escritores, y propaga lo que piensan.

Why Translate into Hñähñu?

Raymundo Isidro Alavez

My interest in translating into my mother tongue, Hñähñu, stems from my desire to share important works I have read and, in so doing, practise my own writing skills in Hñähñu since my language has been passed down in its oral form, with very little in writing. Until very recently, that is, when a few basic texts were produced for teaching purposes. The translations I have undertaken are meant for the vast and diverse population in the many regions where my native tongue is spoken (parts of Hidalgo and the state of Mexico, Querétaro, Guanajuato, Veracruz, Puebla, and a few communities in Michoacán and Tlaxcala).

The identity of Hñähñu culture has been eroded over the years since we were never taught about our culture and have never seen our history highlighted. That is why I became interested in translating *Visión de los vencidos* [published in English as *The Broken Spears; the Aztec Account of the Conquest of Mexico* (Boston: Beacon Press, 1992)] by Dr. Miguel León-Portilla, which is seen as an epic poem on the history of the bravery of the Otomí military leaders during the Spanish conquest. The term "Otomí" was thrust on us by the Náhuatl culture, but those of us from the ethnic group in question call ourselves Ñähñu and our language Hñähñu.

A people's cultural traits are preserved through traditions, which over time incorporate new practices imposed by modern society since traditions are continually evolving. Cultures change, just as societies do, in keeping with the law of dialectics whereby nothing is forever and everything is in flux, except certain societal outcomes and the vestiges of architectural works that remain in our collective memory.

In the world of science, in day-to-day life and the working environment, whatever one person knows has been acquired from others. Language was created to encompass and describe with certainty all that the earth holds. Through prodigious ability, skill and virtue in understanding and imagining issues of importance, translators serve as intermediaries conveying ideas to readers so they may understand them. Thus, translators become innovators, changing vocabulary and creating terms to convey the writers' words and thoughts.

El literato es el resultado de las circunstancias que le toca vivir en su tiempo y espacio, es producto de la cultura en la que se desenvuelve, y también es constructor de conocimientos y trasmisor de valores que quiere inculcar. Al escribir un escritor instruye, trasmite sus emociones, y sentimientos al mismo tiempo. Elabora su lenguaje más adecuado para divulgar lo que desea transmitir.

Reza un dicho popular que las palabras son el espejo del alma. Las clementes palabras manifiestan la calidad humana de quienes las escriben y las pronuncian. El uso del lenguaje permite crear el ambiente en que se vive. Se dice que es arriesgado representar paraísos, cuando lo que domina en el medio ambiente son las privaciones.

Cuando el hombre no se sujeta a un idioma o lengua autóctona se disipa la posibilidad de pensar en entornos de nuestro paisaje, se encubre el contexto circundante, pero también se cierra una puerta a lo imperecedero.

Para el hombre de letras, el lenguaje es la herramienta insustituible para transmitir experiencias, para explicarse a sí mismo, para transmitir los mensajes a los lectores. Los hombres pueden transmitir sus experiencias en conversaciones, pero lo que permanece lo hace a través de la letra escrita. Por eso, debe ser de una forma que pueda ser entendida por casi todos.

En nuestro caso, la lengua hñähñu traslada a los lectores a otra realidad, nombra la fauna, la flora, y los elementos vitales con sus términos propios. Poner un nombre a los objetos y organismos es dar vida a lo inerte, por ello, al igual que otras lenguas autóctonas en el mundo, estos términos deben vivir indefinidamente porque son parte de su identidad comunitaria.

La pertenencia a una cultura tiene su origen en la familia, en la raza, como la señala el ensayista, narrador y poeta de origen maya, Jorge Miguel Cocom Pech, en su inspirado "La casa de tu alma": "Tu idioma es la casa de tu alma/ ahí viven tus padres y tus abuelos/ en esa casa milenarià, hogar de tus recuerdos, permanecen tus palabras, por eso, no llores la muerte de tu cuerpo, ni llores la muerte de tu alma; tu cuerpo, permanece en el rostro de tus hijos, tu alma, eternece en el fulgor de las estrellas".

Los poetas, narradores, novelistas e historiadores escriben en el idioma en que sienten que lo hacen mejor. Quien traduce de un idioma a otro lo hace porque se deleita al leer los escritos, participa en su recreación ; lo que mueve al traductor es dar a conocer esas representaciones de otra cultura, con otro perfil de pensamiento. En la traducción de una obra se

Writers are the product of their circumstances, as well as of their time and place and of the culture in which they evolve. They are also creators of knowledge and conveyers of values they hope to share. In writing, they both educate and convey their emotions and sentiments. They develop the language best suited to revealing what they wish to convey. According to the popular adage, words are the mirror of the soul. Words of mercy demonstrate the humanity of those who write and speak them. The use of language makes it possible to create the environment in which we live. It is said that there is danger in pretending all is paradise when the reigning environment is one of privation.

When we do not hold on to our indigenous languages, we dissipate the possibility of reflecting on our place in the landscape, shroud the surrounding context and close a door to the undying. For a man of letters, language is an irreplaceable tool for conveying experience, discovering oneself, communicating with readers. Humans may relate their experiences to each other in conversations, but what remains is what is written. That is why it must be written in a way that can be understood by almost everyone.

In our case, the Hñähñu language transports readers into another reality, using its own words to name flora, fauna and life forces. For the Ñähñu, to name objects and organisms is to breathe life into what is inert. Thus, as in other indigenous languages throughout the world, those objects and organisms will live on indefinitely since they are part of the community's identity.

To belong to a culture, one must first belong to a family and a nation, as was pointed out by the Mayan essayist, prose writer and poet Jorge Miguel Cocom Pech in his inspiring "La casa de tu alma" [The House of Your Soul]. "Your language is the house of your soul/ therein live your parents and grandparents/ in the millenial home, housing your memories/ your words remain/ and so, do not weep at the death of your body or of your soul/ your body is found in your children's faces/ your soul lives on in the brilliance of the stars."

Poets, storytellers, novelists and historians write in the language in which they feel best able to express themselves. Translators translate from one language to another for the pleasure of what is read and to take part in its re-creation. Translators are motivated by the desire to share representations of other cultures, other patterns of thought. A translation must

evita reducir los mensajes a su sentido literal; se busca el sentido que requiere la frase o la oración que es lo que de verdad importa para describir la obra del literato.

El reto que tiene quien esto escribe es traducir a los notables de la literatura mexicana y algunos de otras latitudes, para encontrar las palabras idóneas en la lengua hñähñu. Este trabajo es grato porque permite construir términos basados en la raíz gramatical de los ya existentes, encontrar en mi lengua la entonación de las palabras, ensanchar el lenguaje para alcanzar una expresión original. Estoy consciente de que no es una empresa fácil pero existe la voluntad para realizarla.

El motivo de este traductor para trasladar una obra a otra lengua es la concordancia con el pensamiento del autor. Escritor y traductor tienen simbolismos afines. Hay similitudes bien marcadas en sus pensamientos, los mismos objetivos que cumplir y coincidencias para divulgar sus ideas entre los lectores.

Lo que este traductor toma en cuenta es la coherencia de las obras literarias, tener afinidad con el estilo del autor, la solidez de sus aseveraciones e investigaciones y, sobre todo, la precisión de la palabra empleada. Estos son los elementos que me llevaron a traducir la obra de Juan Rulfo titulada *El llano en llamas*. Los relatos de este libro están escritos con sencillez, con un vocabulario ágil y, sobre todo, con términos utilizados en la provincia.

La lengua hñähñu es una lengua poética, las expresiones que se emiten en ella van a la esencia de las formas, crean una realidad alterna. Prueba de ello es la irradiación del poeta ñähñu Serafín Thaayrohyadi:

"Sólo vine a suspirar"

"No para siempre florecerán mis ramas/ si llega la sequía y se va el verdor/ sólo vine a estar un momento/ no para siempre estaré despierto// Mis hojas caerán en el viento/ se derrumbará el adobe/ sólo un momento en el vientre/ sólo un momento el arco iris// Sólo vine a cortar leña / sólo a sembrar trébol/ sólo a secar tus lágrimas/ sólo a arrancar espinas venimos// No para siempre humearán las chozas/ no para siempre estaré sangrando/ no para siempre miraré tus labios/ sólo vine a suspirar por ti."

avoid reducing the message to its literal sense; translators strive to render the meaning of words or speech, the essence of the writer's work.

The challenge I face in translating classics from the literature of Mexico and other latitudes is finding the right words in Hñähñu. The task is rewarding in that it leads me to create new terms from existing grammatical roots, finding in my own language the words' intonation, pushing the language even further to come up with original expressions. I know full well the difficulty of the enterprise, but there is no lack of resolve to see it through.

My motivation in bringing a work of literature into another language is whether the author's ideas resonate. Both writer and translator draw on closely related symbolism. There are marked similarities in their thinking as well as in their goals and a shared desire to bring ideas to readers.

What I as a translator take into account is the coherence of a literary work, my affinity for the author's style, the groundedness of the author's assertions and research, and, especially, the precision of the words he chooses. Those same elements led me to translate Juan Rulfo's *El llano en llamas*. The stories included in the collection are related simply, with versatile vocabulary and, most of all, terms used in my region.

Hñähñu is a poetic language. Its expressions go to the very essence of form; they create an alternative reality as can be seen in the luminous work of the Hñähñu poet Serafín Thaayrohyadi:

[Translation in English:]

"I Came Only to Sigh"

My branches will not flower forever/ in times of drought all that is green will disappear/ I came only to stay a while/ I will not always be awake// My leaves will fall on the wind/ my abode will crumble away/ only a moment in the womb/only a moment the rainbow// I came only to chop some wood/ only to sow trefoil/ only to dry your tears/ only to remove poisoned thorns// Smoke will not always rise from the huts/ I will not always bleed/ I will not always gaze on your lips/ I came only to sigh for you.

La traducción al hñähñu :

« **Sehe da ehe ga ngätsi** »

Inga nzäi da ndoni ma y'eza/ nub'u da tsoho ra ñ'ot'i da ma ra nk'ami/sehe da ehe n'a n'amitho/inga nzäi ga nuhu// Ma xi da dagi ha ra ndähi/ da yot'e ra k'ohai/ sehe n'a n'amitho ha ra debi/ sehe n'a n'amitho ra begri// Sehe da ehe ga heki ra za/ sehe da ehe ga pot'i ra xero/ sehe ga ot'i ri gida/ sehe ga k'utsi ya b'ini da ehehu// Inga nzäi da mfuni ya zengu/ inga nzäi da bonga ma ji/ inga nzäi ga handi ri xine/ sehe da ehe ga ngätsi po nge'i.

La lengua hñahñu concibe en forma distinta al hombre y a la mujer. En el caso de ella, su habla aprecia en forma distinta la realidad, por eso utiliza términos con distintas resonancias que son más dúctiles, en tanto que el hombre pronuncia las palabras más fuerte. Suavidad y fuerza se complementan. Ejemplo de ello, para decir muchacho la mujer pronuncia "metsi" el hombre dice "ts'unt'u", la primera para decir hombre es "däme" y el segundo es "ñ'oho".

Todas las áreas del conocimiento han sufrido modificaciones originadas por el uso del vocabulario; éste cambia en forma permanente de acuerdo a las circunstancias e inventos tecnológicos. Algunos términos han sido desplazados por otros más actuales y eso es normal como lo distingue un fragmento poético: "Todos cambiamos cada día que pasa" "El río pasa, pasa. / Nunca cesa / El viento pasa, pasa/ Nunca cesa.// Nunca regresa". "Gatho di mponihu tat'a pa ge thogi/ Ra däthe thogi, thogi/ inham'u ri k'atsi/ ra ndähi thogi, thogi/ hnham'u ri k'atsi// inham'u pengi."(Garribay Kintana 238-239)

Los hombres productores de conocimientos, manifestados en las artes (pintura, letras, música, poesía y arquitectura), han dejado y siguen dejando constancia escrita, obras pictóricas, obras materiales: utensilios de labranza, vestimenta, armas. Ellos siguen siendo los protectores de las tradiciones; algunas de ellas han entrado en competitividad permanente para establecer un modelo de vida, son pocas las que se han impuesto. Otras han desaparecido, pero al desaparecer las tradiciones desaparecen las culturas. Este término es conceptualizado por el incansable investigador de la cultura hñähñu, Dr. David Charles Wright Carr: "La cultura puede definirse como las ideas, valores y los patrones de conducta de cada grupo humano. Ésta se adapta a los cambios geográficos, políticos y sociales."

The translation into Hñähñu :

« Sehe da ehe ga ngätsi »

Inga nzäi da ndoni ma y'eza/ nub'u da tsoho ra ñ'ot'i da ma ra nk'ami/sehe da
ehe n'a n'amitho/inga nzäi ga nuhu// Ma xi da dagi ha ra ndähi/ da yot'e ra
k'ohai/ sehe n'a n'amitho ha ra debi/ sehe n'a n'amitho ra begri// Sehe da ehe
ga heki ra za/ sehe da ehe ga pot'i ra xero/ sehe ga ot'i ri gida/ sehe ga k'utsi
ya b'ini da ehehu// Inga nzäi da mfuni ya zengu/ inga nzäi da bonga ma ji/
inga nzäi ga handi ri xine/ sehe da ehe ga ngätsi po nge'i.

The Hñähñu language conceives of men and women differently. When
speaking, women translate reality differently, hence the language they use
is more pliable, while men use words more forcefully. Gentleness and force
serve to complement each other. One example is that a woman will use the
word *metsi* for "boy" while a man will use *ts'unt'u*. A woman will use *däme* for
"man" while a man will use *ñ'oho*.

All areas of knowledge have undergone change that is reflected in their
vocabulary, which is in a state of permanent flux subject to circumstances
and technological inventions. Some terms have been replaced by other,
more up-to-date expressions, a normal occurrence as described in the
following excerpt from the poem "We All Change With Each New Day":
"The river runs and runs/ it never stops/ the wind blows and blows/
it never stops/ it never turns back." "Gatho di mponihu tat'a pa ge thogi/
Ra däthe thogi, thogi/ inham'u ri k'atsi/ ra ndähi thogi, thogi/ hnham'u
ri k'atsi// inham'u pengi." (Garribay Kintana 238-239)

In producing knowledge as seen in the arts (painting, literature, music,
poetry and architecture), humans leave behind written records, works
of art, artifacts: tools, clothing and weapons. They continue to safeguard
sometimes competing traditions—some trying to impose their lifestyle
and a very few managing to do so. Others disappear, but as traditions
disappear, so do cultures. Culture itself has been described by Dr. David
Charles Wright Carr, a tireless researcher into the Hñähñu culture, as
follows: "Culture can be defined as the ideas, values and patterns of
behaviour of each human group. Culture adapts to geographic,
political and social change."

La lengua hablada y escrita es un agente elemental de la cultura, que le sirve para su propia preservación. En todos los idiomas existen desacuerdos, porque difieren en sus sonidos y significado de las cosas, e igualmente en las regiones en donde éstos se hablan, porque se distinguen las variantes, mas nunca esas diferencias lingüísticas implican diferencias culturales. En cada región existe multiplicidad lingüística, pero en su conjunto no hay diferencias abismales.

El planeta tierra presenta una biodiversidad que se asemeja a la de la sociedad. En ella existe una pluralidad lingüística y multiculturalidad, es decir, coexisten diferentes culturas en un mismo país o región. Asimismo hay una interrelación entre las lenguas, es decir, una interculturalidad. No hay supremacía de unos y sumisión de otros ; existen en condiciones de igualdad. Así, como no hay una cultura superior tampoco hay una cultura inferior, sólo son diferentes.

Todas las culturas conservan una historia amplia y profunda. Sin embargo, la invaluable riqueza en arte, en emotivas canciones y poesía, en obras de teatro, en laboriosas artesanías y arquitectura, en exquisitas destrezas culinarias, podría perderse por la veloz globalización que pone en riesgo a las miles de culturas que se encuentran diseminadas en todo el mundo.

The spoken and written language is a fundamental agent for a culture's preservation. There are divisions within all languages due to varying sounds and meanings; the same holds true within regions because of different language variants, however, linguistic differences do not imply cultural differences. Each region enjoys linguistic multiplicity, yet with no gaping differences overall.

The biodiversity of planet Earth is like the linguistic and multicultural plurality of society; that is, different cultures co-exist within the same country or region. There is also an interconnectedness among languages, interculturality as it were. There is no supremacy of a few and submission of the rest; they exist in conditions of equality. There is no superior or inferior culture, only differences.

All cultures have a rich, deep history. Nevertheless, the invaluable wealth of art, stirring songs and poems, works of theatre, handicrafts, architectural masterpieces and exquisite culinary skill could all be lost in the race to globalization that endangers the thousands of cultures spread throughout the world.

Translation by S. Ouriou

Not Making It Up: the Translating Writer
Medeine Tribinevičius

One night at BILTC I was on the phone with a writer friend. I was telling him about the residency, about what I was working on and he asked me, tongue firmly in cheek: "How do they know you're not just making it all up?"

Indeed—how would anyone know? I translate from a "minor" language—there are only an estimated 4 to 5 million Lithuanian speakers in the world. How can most people be sure that the pages of English text I churn out are actually faithful representations of the original? This is a bit of a ridiculous question—as part of the ethics of translation, one adheres to certain rules, of which an important one is to translate what is written, not what you think should have been written.

My friend was teasing me about the obscure nature of what I do, but his comment made me think about something else. How can I be sure that my other day job—that of "the writer" —is not interfering with the integrity of the text? Is it possible to keep the writer separate from the translator? And what about the converse—do other writers' texts find their way into my own work?

There is necessarily an intimate relationship between translator and writer. And I don't think that the question of where the translator ends and the writer begins is one that is easily answered. A translator is a writer—we read, re-read, write, re-write, edit, re-write, edit, re-write, edit, send it off for proofreading and, yes, you guessed it, editing. We research the work we're translating—the context, history, intertextual references. We make creative choices about voice, diction, pacing, word usage, punctuation. We pay as much attention to the text as the writer does, sometimes even more (I know I've asked writers what they meant by certain phrases, sentences or words only to have them answer, "It sounded good." I'm also guilty of the same as a writer.) A translator uses the same techniques and tools as a writer. We engage in an analogous process—transmitting a world from the page into the mind of a reader.

But what about the opposite—is a writer a translator? A writer translates ideas, experiences, emotions into texts, but just as translation is not simply transplanting meaning into another language, (good) writing is not

organizing facts and events in some order. They are both interpretive processes, arts, and it is at this important juncture that my writer-self meets my translator-self.

As I writer I am deeply and unavoidably influenced by the translation work I do, and I cannot imagine that the interaction could work in one direction only. In both instances, be it translation work or the creation of my own texts, I have an intimate relationship with the material. I remember the first literary work I translated: a series of poems by Lithuanian poet and filmmaker Jonas Mekas. I wanted to share them with a friend who at the time was obsessed with Mekas' films. What I found was that the translation process, with all its restrictions related to form and content, was in fact liberating. It brought me to text and writing from a different angle and removed some of the pressure to create an original text (though I do believe that each translated text is an original text).

Translation, for me, is one of the best writing exercises there is. It allows me to try on another voice, forces me into genres that I may not have thought about trying before and allows me to examine the inner mechanics of a piece of writing. It's like trying on another writer's shoes and going for a walk, and if all goes well, taking them out for a night on the town. This type of experimentation, with all its restrictions, demands another kind of creativity and feeds the writing process. A good example of this is the project I was working on at BILTC, the translation of a novel called *Tūla*. I fell in love with the book while living in Vilnius. I chose this particular book because it captures the mystical qualities of the city of Vilnius, appeals to my personal experiences in the city and is one of the best books, in my estimation, coming out of Lithuania in the post-Independence period. But just as the translator in me fell in love with the text, so did the writer. Elements of *Tūla* have found their way into my own work. I've experimented with magic realism, explored ways of layering history into a text and discovered surprising juxtaposed images all because I spent so much time immersed in the translation of another text.

As a translator from a "minor" language, I often find myself employed in a third job: the position of cultural ambassador. People ask me about the writing scene in Lithuania, or to recommend some poets or novelists; they want to discuss current trends and influences. And I'm happy to do this, but mostly because I'm engaged with the Lithuanian literary community

on several levels—as a translator, as a writer and as part of the Lithuanian émigré community. However, as much as I am part of the Lithuanian community, I am also an outsider, a position that includes one very important duty—being an ambassador for the English language. One key feature of the Lithuanian writing community is that many writers are also translators and because the country was closed to Western influence for so many years, many great works of contemporary Western literature (in particular in English) are only now being translated. The Beat poets, for example, 20th century writers from the United States, even Dante, whose Inferno was translated to great acclaim just two years ago. As a result of this recent increase in translation, I have worked with many writer-translators in Lithuania as an editor and as a point of reference for anything from New York slang to contemporary Native American life and literature. And of course, every time I cross the Atlantic, I haul a suitcase of books with me to add to the libraries of my Lithuanian writer friends.

So to come back to the initial question: is it possible to separate the writer from the translator and vice versa? My answer is sure, probably, with some effort, but really, why would you want to? The translating writer is connected to a long and living tradition of writers who translate and translators who write. Separating the two is hard work. Drawing on the adage that two heads are better than one, in this case two languages, feeding into one another, and two literary traditions interacting, are certainly more exciting and innovative.

Fragments of a Greater Language

Katharina Rout

How can I translate into a language that remains puzzling and challenging to me? I translate contemporary German-language fiction into English, a language I speak with the echo of my native German and a sprinkling of strange New Zealand words acquired from my husband. "All translation is only a somewhat provisional way of coming to terms with the foreignness of languages," Walter Benjamin taught us in "The Task of the Translator." I worry about accents and effacements and am humbled in my longing to produce a translation shot through with the beauty of the original. Nevertheless, the act of translating gives me great joy and satisfaction. "Glory be to God for dappled things," —I comfort myself with Gerald Manley Hopkins's "Pied Beauty" in moments of doubt— "for skies of couple-colour as a brinded cow..."

Each of the novels I have translated challenges stylistic and linguistic norms. The syntax of Marlene Streeruwitz's *Seductions* is as fragmented as its protagonist's life and as subversive of grammatical norms as its author is of conventional gender relations. From her truncated sentences I moved to the opposite: long, generously hospitable sentences in Ulla Berkéwicz's *Love in a Time of Terror* that made room for echoes of eight languages and a multi-ethnic cast of characters, for a range of sexual orientations and the wisdom of several world religions, for quotations from Spinoza and Heine, and references to Tchaikovksy and Brahms. In a globalized world, Berkéwicz's novel suggests, languages have to open themselves to the other, and translation becomes a moral and political necessity.

For some time now, I have been translating Galsan Tschinag's autobiographical fiction from an idiosyncratic German that is dappled and accented as no other. This Mongolian writer, whose name in his native Tuvan language is Irgit Shynykbaj-oglu Dshurukuvaa and who in "The Story of Names" tells of the fifteen names he has been given in a plethora of languages, is a linguistic and cultural go-between. A transnational writer, he divides his time between Mongolia's capital Ulaanbataar, his Tuvan homeland in the High Altai mountains in remote western Mongolia, and Germany, the country whose language he has adopted for most of his works. Fluent in six languages, he is multilingual and—today with publications in both German and Mongolian—he is what theorists call an ambilingual

translingual writer. Most significantly for me, he is a translator, and not only because he has translated German literature into Mongolian.

When Tschinag was born in the early 1940s into a family of nomadic herders, his native Tuvan was an oral language with rich epic traditions but no script. At his Mongolian-language boarding school, the young Galsan encounters letters for the first time, and they remind him of animal tracks in the snow. Soon he learns Mongolian, Kazakh and Russian, and the altered state of adolescence awakens his poetic and shamanic gifts.

He writes poems by the hundreds and decides to become a second Mikhail Lermontov. Lermontov's translation of Goethe's "Wayfarer's Night Song" leaves him spellbound though he remains unaware of Goethe's nationality, fame, or other works. Years later, now a university student in Leipzig, East Germany, Tschinag recognizes the poet's name, first seen in Cyrillic letters, when his German-language teacher introduces him to Goethe's poem "Heidenröslein." He's heard the name before! On the spot he translates Lermontov's translation into German, and the teacher recognizes the poem. It will still take years before Tschinag starts writing in German, with an implicit gesture we might today consider post-colonial, of rejecting Mongolian and Russian. Decades later, in an unpublished essay on his life-long veneration of Goethe, he describes Goethe as a shaman. The triptych over his desk in Ulaanbaatar shows a photo of the sacred Haarakan Mountain in the Altai as its centre piece and, to the right and left, pictures of the two shamans whom Tschinag venerates the most apart from his shaman teacher, his Aunt Pürvü: Goethe and Beethoven.

I am moved that a poem translated into Russian by a poet from the Caucasus, memorized and translated back into German by a Tuvan student from Mongolia, should carry such powerful echoes of the original. It gives me hope that the translatability of Tschinag's works allows them to wander the world and survive the passage through my translations. Poetry is not what gets lost in translation but what is retained. Tschinag writes German with a Tuvan accent, grateful for the gift of German literature and Goethe in particular and enriching the German language in the process with markers of his indigenous culture's oral tradition, its parataxis and frequent use of alliteration and assonance reminiscent of stave rhyme. Similarly, I try to give something back to English literature when I translate his wondrous German into the hospitable English of my chosen country. To quote Benjamin again, "translation does not find itself in the center of the language forest but on the outside facing the wooded ridge; it calls into it without

entering, aiming at that single spot where the echo is able to give, in its own language, the reverberation of the work in the alien one."

Tschinag's work is full of echoes itself. The writer regards his works not as his individual creation but as the collective works of his people that he gives voice to. His people, the tiny and threatened Tuvan minority in Mongolia, revere him as their chieftain and shaman and call him their singer, and he is a bard in the epic tradition, or a story-teller as Benjamin described that role. When Tschinag writes his people's stories, he translates: from oral experience into literacy, and from a Turkic language in which pitch matters—two systems of vowel harmony exist, and sounds are soft and round like the nomads' felted yurts—into a hissing Germanic language whose sounds are square and hard-edged like German brick houses. How can I hope to capture these layers in my English translations? I keep wondering how much I have to give up of his German in hopes of reaching back to his Tuvan—a language I do not speak from a country for which I have only an outsider's appreciation. "A literary translator is bilingual and bicultural and thus inhabits a landscape which is not mapped by conventional geographies; s/he is at home in the flux that is the reality of contemporary culture, where migration is constant across artificial political boundaries," writes Peter Bush in the *Routledge Encyclopedia of Translation Studies* ("Literary Translation: Practices"). I need not a bilateral, but a multilateral frame of reference. Moving on horseback and camel through the nomadic world of the Tuvans helped me to better understand Tschinag's writing, as did eating their food and drinking their fermented mares' milk. More importantly, I experienced how the Tuvan world, too, is in great flux and undergoing dramatic changes. Survival requires bending with the storms of change and making do with imperfections—and learning to appreciate "all things counter, original, spare, strange, [...] fickle [and] freckled." And so I work on my strange translations trusting that the Tuvan voice will leave enough of an echo even in my English, thrice removed, and that, to quote Benjamin again, "both the original and the translation [are] recognizable as fragments of a greater language."

In his 2008 novel *Die Rückkehr: Roman meines Lebens* [The Return: The Novel of My Life] Tschinag tells of moving back to his people and their homeland in the Altai, and describes a selfless and bold act of translation that is infinitely encouraging to me. Ak and Gök, an aged couple, welcome Tschinag not with the traditional gifts of cheese or drink but with a stack of loose-leafed paper, covered in text written in different, inexperi-

enced hands. The couple has learned that Tuvan children, in a sharp reversal of the assimilative practices of previous decades, are now being taught their language at school (Tschinag, in fact, has been instrumental in creating and funding the Tuvan school). However, the Tuvan that these students learn sounds strange and awkward to Ak and Gök, and it is: in the absence of local reading material, the school has resorted to print material from the Republic of Tyva. In the 1930s, a Buddhist monk had devised the first writing system, a Latin-based alphabet, for the People's Republic of Tuva (as it was called then); in 1941, the monk was executed in a Stalinist purge; and in 1943, Russian linguists with no knowledge of Tuvan replaced his script with a Cyrillic script which is still in use today but remains a poor fit. Ak and Gök decided that the Mongolian Tuvan children needed to learn from material reflecting their own language and culture. Though illiterate, the couple knew many stories, and so they organized paper and pen and paid school children with candy and chewing gum to write down their stories. When they discovered that Tschinag himself had published some fiction and poetry in Mongolian, they found people who read his works to them until they had memorized the texts; found others who were more fluently bilingual and could help them translate; and finally, found students who would write their translations down in Tuvan. Riddled with misunderstandings, clumsy and imprecise, these translations into an essentially still oral language challenge the fate of a minority language and culture. They will forever be dearest to him, Tschinag writes, more precious than any other translation of his works into any other language.

I remember this story with gratitude as I struggle at my laptop with my own flawed translation. "Glory be to God for dappled things .... and all trades, their gear and tackle and trim."

Translating Poetry

**bey
on
d
wo
rds**

Translating
the World

Buscando una voz gemela:
Traducir y cantar los poemas de Lorna Crozier
Carmen Leñero

> *Mon inspiration n'est pas verbale.*
> *Elle ne procède pas par mots*
> *plutôt par formes musicales.*
>
> Paul Valéry, Cahiers

La primera lectura: escuchar el poema

Hay quienes vivimos la poesía como una forma de conciencia pero
también como una forma de respiración, sin la cual nuestra existencia
carecería de sentido. En la penumbra de mi estudio, sentada bajo una
lámpara de lectura, voy recorriendo los poemas de Lorna Crozier,
escritos en un inglés directo, sugestivo y musical. Su voz femenina llena
mi oído interno. Sus paisajes y minúsculas escenas cotidianas invaden mi
mente e iluminan zonas que nunca he visitado, pero que me son extraña-
mente familiares. Me dejo llevar por la cadencia de los versos, como si me
pertenecieran, como si los conociera de memoria, y de pronto fuese
descubriendo aquello que residía desde siempre dentro de mí.

> **Nunca me sentí tan desconectada**
> **de todo. Luz y su ausencia.**
> **Lluvia. El gato en el alféizar cazando moscas.**
> **Glenn Gould tocando Las variaciones Goldberg**
> **por última vez.**
> **Las infinitas variaciones de ti,**
> **haciendo el café, escogiendo semillas para el jardín,**
> **invitándome a subir para el amor... (164,165)**

Cuando Lorna Crozier escribe estos versos incluidos en su poemario
Angels of Flesh, Angels of Silence, está escuchando la última interpretación
grabada que hizo Glenn Gould de "Las variaciones Goldberg".
La escucha resonar por el ambiente, un día cualquiera, y siente deseos
de "cantar" en el silencio del papel sus propias "variaciones" de la pieza.
La música flotante de Bach se funde con la presencia cotidiana de su
amante y con la voz secreta de los objetos que la rodean, allí en su casa de
Victoria, mientras, afuera, llueve. Crozier traduce esa experiencia íntegra
en un poema que, pese a ser sólo escritura, contiene implícita su propia
"música callada". El poema nació de la escucha y genera a su vez un nuevo
espacio de escucha para los lectores.

Seeking a Twin Voice:
Translating and Singing Lorna Crozier's Poems

Carmen Leñero

Mon inspiration n'est pas verbale.
Elle ne procède pas par mots
plutôt par formes musicales.

Paul Valéry, Cahiers

First reading: listening to the poem

Some of us experience poetry as a form of awareness, of breath even,
without which our existence would be meaningless. In the shadows of my
den, seated by a reading lamp, I thumb through Lorna Crozier's poems
written in an English that is direct, suggestive and musical. Her feminine
voice fills my inner ear. Her landscapes and miniature scenes from daily
life flood my mind and highlight areas I had never before visited, but
which nonetheless seem strangely familiar. I let myself be buoyed by the
cadence of the verses, as though they belong to me, as though I know them
by heart, and in no time I discover that which has always lived in me.

> **Never have I felt so unconnected**
> **to everything. Light and its absence.**
> **Rain. The cat on the windowsill catching flies.**
> **Glenn Gould playing the Goldberg Variations**
> **his last time.**
> **The endless variations of you**
> **making coffee, ordering seeds for the garden,**
> **calling me upstairs to love . . .**

Crozier wrote these verses for her collection *Angels of Flesh, Angels of Silence*
while listening to the last recording Glenn Gould made of "The Goldberg
Variations." One day, hearing the way it resonated, she felt the desire to
"sing" to the silence of paper her own "variations" on the piece. Bach's
floating music becomes one with the daily presence of her lover and the
secret voice of the objects surrounding her in her Victoria home as rain
falls outside. Crozier translates the entire experience in a poem that,
although written, not sung, has its own implicit "silent music." The poem
was born from listening and, in turn, birthed a new kind of listening
for readers.

Así pues, cuando leo, sentada en mi estudio de la Ciudad de México, escucho en mi mente la cadencia del poema, en contrapunto con la memoria que guardo de la pieza de Bach y la interpretación de Gould que conozco bien, mientras el calor absorbido por las paredes de mi casa durante las horas diurnas se libera y me envuelve. Aquí no llueve ni hace frío, y estoy a solas, pero la vivencia de la poeta se traslada hasta mi cuerpo, como si yo fuera un instrumento musical y sus palabras teclearan sobre mí:

> **Los dedos de Gould sobre teclas de marfil.**
> **No es Bach lo que interpreta**
> **desde la tumba, corazón en pausa.**
> **Tan libre de gravedad la mente asciende**
> **como una semilla alada, apenas**
> **contenida en una cáscara ligera.**
> **No es Bach, sino música aun antes de tener**
> **la más mínima huella humana.**
>   **¿Es esto el éxtasis?,**
> **¿esta extraña sensación de lejanía? Tan distante**
> **cae la lluvia. Las variaciones de Gould**
> **a Goldberg. Tus manos. El frío,**
> **frío azul. Mi piel.**

La experiencia que funda el poema de Crozier está compuesta por varias capas de percepción en concierto, elocuentes de una forma inédita. En medio del silencio y la penumbra en que me encuentro, la interpretación de Glenn Gould, que escucho sólo en mi memoria, se sintoniza con las sonoridades verbales de un idioma que me es ajeno (el inglés) y con la musicalidad creada por la cadencia y ritmo de los versos de este poema en particular. Su musicalidad hecha de memoria y sorpresa vibra, pues, en mis huesos y me produce además un efecto de elevación, incluso si el significado de algunas frases se me escapa. Antes de ser capaz de comprender los alcances de cada imagen o el significado preciso de cada expresión, ya habito el poema como una atmósfera acústica y emocional y adopto el ritmo del pensamiento que suscita. Aspiro el poema igual que una aroma suave, penetrante, que me llega sin embargo desde muy lejos.

Balbuceo en español algunos versos sueltos: "esta extraña sensación de lejanía" (*this strange remoteness*). La lluvia. Los dedos de Gould sobre teclas de marfil (*ivory keys*). Pronuncio en voz alta "ivory keys". Fonéticamente, la expresión suena en mis oídos como: "letras precisas", "gotas lujosas", "joyas", acentos cristalinos en el aire que respiro. *Ivory keys* es una sensación en la yema de mis dedos, la de pulsar palabras en un piano invisible, la de resbalar suavemente por la escala, como si esquiara por la nieve, como si lamiera los sonidos...

Thus, when I read it seated in my den in Mexico City, I hear in my mind the cadence of the poem as counterpoint to the memory I retain of Bach's piece and Gould's interpretation that I know so well, while the heat absorbed by the walls of my home during the daylight hours rises and envelops me. Here it is neither raining nor cold, I am alone, but the poet's aliveness conveys itself to my body, as though I were a musical instrument being played by her words:

> Gould's fingers on ivory keys.
> It isn't Bach he's playing
> from the grave, the stopped heart.
> So free of gravity the mind lifts
> like a feathered seed, only
> a thin shell of bone holding it in.
> Not Bach, but music before it became
> the least bit human.
>   Is this ecstasy,
> this strange remoteness? Rain falling
> from such a distance. Gould's Goldberg
> Variations. Your hands. The cold
> cold blue. My skin.

The experience that gave rise to Crozier's poem is a concert of various layers of perception, eloquent in its originality. Surrounded by silence and shadows as I am, the Glenn Gould interpretation I hear in memory melds with the verbal sonority of a language foreign to me (English) and with the musicality created by the cadence and rhythm of the verses of the poem itself. Its musicality, made of memory and surprise, thrums in my bones, lifting me up, even when the meaning of certain lines escapes me. Already, before understanding the outer reaches of each image or the exact meaning of each expression, I dwell in the poem as though in an acoustic and emotional ambience and adopt the rhythm of thought it creates. I breathe in the poem the way I would a sweet, penetrating scent wafting to me from afar.

I take a stab at a few random verses in Spanish: "this strange remoteness." The rain. Gould's fingers on ivory keys. I say "ivory keys" out loud. Phonetically, the expression sounds to my ears like : "letras precisas" [precise letters], "gotas lujosas" [luxurious drops], "joyas" [jewels], crystalline accents in the air I breathe. "Ivory keys" is a sensation in my fingertips, of sounding words on an invisible piano along a gently ascending scale, like skiing through snow, licking sound...

Mientras ensayo a musitar en castellano ciertas líneas del poema y me sumerjo en la labor de encontrar los adjetivos adecuados o las frases que logren traducir la idea exacta de esos verbos tan precisos y sintéticos que abundan en inglés, voy huyendo de la rima. Esa rima pegajosa que tan fácilmente se impone en español cuando uno se coloca en actitud de escribir un poema. Y busco más bien en la frescura de la prosa el tono exacto que se asimile al estilo directo y coloquial de la poeta.

Hay pocas rimas en la poesía de Crozier. Su música radica en la acentuación, en la recurrencia de cierta vocal y en el trayecto auditivo que ésta va trazando a lo largo del poema. No hay estribillos ni patrones fijos en sus líneas; hay una pausada forma de moverse desde lo visible hacia lo invisible, de ida y vuelta, como si se tratara de una operación natural y espontánea. ¿Cómo puedo caminar estas mismas trayectorias con mis propias palabras mexicanas y los giros de mi sintaxis española? Dice Lorna Crozier que hay un lenguaje primigenio al que sus versos aspiran, un lenguaje anterior a las distintas lenguas del mundo y a las diferencias culturales, anterior incluso al lenguaje humano. En ese lenguaje primigenio fuimos "alguna vez" capaces de comunicarnos con los animales y las piedras, con el halcón cuyos planeos en el aire generan el cielo o con la libélula que camina "sobre pétalos sin herirlos". Yo le creo. Yo acepto la invitación de su poesía a situarme en esa dimensión del lenguaje, y sólo desde ahí volver al mío... como quien extrae de la maraña de discursos las palabras esenciales: "pan", "sal", "amigo", "luna".

> **Y en la tierra toda una sola lengua
> y un solo hablar. Venado habla con mujer
> mujer con zorro, sin temor ni suspicacia.
> Urraca conversa con rata almizclera, y ¡ah,
> la hierba!, qué húmedo y elocuente
> coloquio verde sostiene con la llovizna.**

Sobre esta posibilidad soñada de aproximarse a la musicalidad primordial de las criaturas, música anterior al lenguaje, meditaba Lorna cuando hablábamos de cómo la traducción de poesía implica moverse en una zona no verbal, intermedia entre dos lenguas.

Pero, ¿habrá en realidad una música corporal y callada, una cadencia virtual previa al poema, previa a la lengua misma, de donde surgen las metáforas más puras? ¿Cómo acceder a esa música primigenia que su oído identifica y darle materialidad en el idioma español? Siendo una poeta "de a pie" reconozco que me encuentro con una poesía que vuela.

As I try to meditate in Spanish on certain lines of the poem and throw myself into the task of finding fitting adjectives or lines to translate the exact idea of the many concise verbs found in English, I distance myself from rhyming—the cloying rhymes that come too easily in Spanish when writing a poem. Instead I look to the freshness of the prose for a tone that will match the poet's direct, colloquial style.

There are very few rhymes in Crozier's poetry. Her music is found in the stresses, in the recurrence of certain vowels and in the auditory trajectory the same vowels trace through the poem. There are no refrains or fixed patterns in its lines, just a measured way of moving from the visible to the invisible, then back again, as though part of a natural, spontaneous occurrence. How can I follow the same trajectories with my own Mexican words and the twists and turns of my Spanish syntax?

For Lorna Crozier, there is a primal language to which her verses aspire, a language anterior to the various languages of the world and to cultural differences, anterior to human language itself. "Once upon a time" we were able to communicate in this primal language with animals and rocks, with the hawk that creates the sky with its soaring wings or the dragon-fly that "walks on petals and leaves no bruise." I believe her. I accept her poetry's invitation to find my place in that dimension of language, and then and only then return to my own . . . like someone extracting from the tide of speech the most essential words: "bread," "salt," "friend," "moon."

> And the whole earth is of one language
> and one speech. Deer talks to woman
> and woman to fox, no mistrust or fear.
> Magpie chats with muskrat, and oh,
> the grass! How wet and eloquent
> its green jive with the rain. (Apocrypha of Light)

When I spoke to Lorna about how translating poetry means moving within a non-verbal zone, an intermediary zone between two languages, Lorna mused on the dreamed-of possibility of drawing closer to the primal musicality of all creatures, a music anterior to language.

However, is there truly a silenced music within the body, a virtual cadence anterior to the poem, anterior to language itself, from which the purest of metaphors arise? How to access the primal music one's ear identifies and give it shape in Spanish? Being an earthbound poet, I recognize that I am in the presence of poetry that soars.

"Debo seguir los giros de Crozier en el aire, me digo; debo imitar esos giros con la voz, con el cuerpo, con el pensamiento y en los terrenos de mi propia ensoñación".

Mientras releo en voz alta los versos de Crozier, siento sobre mi piel el toque fino de su dulzura, la cosquilla de su ironía, el largo aliento de su serenidad, los súbitos vuelcos que permiten a la poeta trenzar lo cotidiano y lo trascendente, lo cercano y lo lejano, su interpretación del mundo, los recuerdos de un corazón y las mil pequeñas cosas que hablan a los oídos de una mujer despierta. Siento, sobre todo, una especie de contagio: el deseo de musitar cada sílaba de esos versos, como si yo también tocara con mi lengua unas teclas invisibles; la tentación de poner sus palabras en mi garganta y desde ahí hacerlas resonar por el aire de mi casa; el anhelo de imprimir sus imágenes en mi voz... y cantar a los cuatro vientos los misterios que me revelan, agradecida de que el poema haya llegado hasta mí desde un punto tan lejano. Quiero, en suma, cantar los versos en esa lengua que no es mía, saborear esas frases con sus extrañas vocales, con su articulación particular, con sus honduras sonoras, su entonación foránea. Aunque mi conocimiento del inglés es limitado, mi cuerpo de poeta se siente arrastrado sensualmente al mundo poético de esta delicada escritora canadiense. Es mi pensamiento musical y táctil el que responde en primera instancia a la poesía de Crozier, igual que un eco, engendrando en mí una voz nueva, una especie de voz gemela, desconocida como un hijo que se lleva en el vientre. Esa voz que va naciendo en mí se forja en la lengua inglesa pero quiere de inmediato reencontrar las sonoridades entrañables de mi lengua madre.

"He de traducir este poema de Lorna, y otros más", me digo en un arranque de voracidad literaria. Pero me contengo: sé bien que la traducción de un texto debe recorrer un arduo y enrevesado camino. Implica un desmenuzamiento racional de los significados, una decodificación del contexto, un análisis casi cruel de las posibilidades que tiene (o que no tiene) cada concepto para trasladarse de un mundo cultural a otro. Y en ese camino áspero, aunque ciertamente interesante, de encontrar "supuestas equivalencias" para los vocablos y los ritmos, temo perder la frescura e integridad de la experiencia primera, mi experiencia de lectora contagiada, poseída por otra voz.

Y sin embargo, me lanzo en ese camino, entusiasmada más por su misterio que por lo que alcanzo a comprender en esta primera lectura, intuitiva y a tientas. Mi labor de traducción comienza, pues, atendiendo a la musicalidad y movimientos internos de los poemas, tal y como se aprende la lengua materna: imitando los sonidos y los gestos, disfrutando la densidad de los

"I must follow Crozier's aerobatics," I tell myself. "I have to imitate them with my voice, my body, my thoughts, even my dreams."

As I re-read aloud Crozier's verses, I feel their soft touch on my own skin, the tickle of their irony, the extended breath of their serenity, the sudden about-turns that allow the poet to weave together the quotidian and the transcendent, the near and the far, her interpretation of the world, heart memories and the thousand small things that speak to the ear of a woman awake. Above all, I feel a sort of contagion: the desire to murmur each syllable of the verses, as though using my tongue on invisible keys; the temptation to place her words in my throat and have them resonate through my house; the desire to imprint her images on my voice . . . and sing to the four winds the mysteries revealed to me there, in gratitude, knowing the great distance the poem has had to cover to reach me. In sum, I want to sing the verses in the language that is not my own, savour the lines with their strange vowels, their particular articulation, their echoing depths, their foreign intonation. Although my knowledge of English is limited, my poet's body feels a sensual pull toward the poetic world of this delicate Canadian writer. My musical and tactile instincts are the first to respond to Crozier's poetry, like an echo, engendering in me a new voice, a sort of twin voice, as unknown as a child in the womb. The voice coming to life in me is forged in the English language but desires nothing more than to draw to it the sonority of my mother tongue.

"I must translate Lorna's poems, this one and the others," I think in a burst of literary voracity. But I hold back: I know any text's translation takes an arduous, winding road. It involves a rational diminishing of the signified, a decoding of context, an almost cruel analysis of the possibilities (existing or no) that will allow each concept to move from one cultural universe to another. On that steep yet surely fascinating path seeking "supposed equivalencies" for the words and rhythms, I am afraid of losing the freshness and integrity of the first experience, its contagion, the being possessed by another voice.

Nevertheless, I start down that road, excited more by its mystery than what I was able to grasp in my first intuitive and tentative reading. The work of translation begins with an ear to the musicality and internal movement of poems, just as one learns a mother tongue: imitating the sounds and gestures, enjoying the density of the words and the flow of their combinations,

vocablos y el flujo de sus combinaciones, ensayando sus esquemas de entonación, entrando en la zona de sensaciones que ese flujo provoca, acogiendo su resonancia anímica y recreando la situación mental en que los sonidos van haciendo sentido. Así por ejemplo, para traducir el poema de Crozier "Miedo a las serpientes" hube de hundirme en aquella "O" silenciosa y aterradora que surge de la boca abierta de una serpiente y culebrea de verso en verso, guiando el desarrollo mismo del poema:

...vimos cómo Larry la clavaba al poste de madera del teléfono.
Ella se retorció entre ambos clavos, gemelos iridiscentes,
incapaz de arrastrarse hacia afuera del dolor,
su boca abierta, la lengua roja paladeando
su propio espanto; la amé entonces,
a esa serpiente. Los chicos ahí parados con sus manos idiotas
colgando de las muñecas, y aquella boca verde
tan hermosa, abriéndose en una O terrible y negra
que nadie podía escuchar.

Escuchar a la naturaleza y darle voz en el poema

Uno de los escritores preferidos de Lorna Crozier, John Berger, decía que "la poesía está en oír." Para ella también la escritura poética no es invención, ni siquiera traducción de una visión íntima, sino ante todo una escucha atenta del mundo, una forma de escuchar la voz de las cosas y las criaturas. Las cosas son sólo lo que son, dice, y para escribir un poema sobre ellas "las cosas mismas me tienen que hablar". No se trata, pues, de manipularlas mentalmente o reconstruirlas; se trata de explorar lo que los animales, los fenómenos y los objetos son capaces de expresar. Hay que descubrir de manera intuitiva y devota las metáforas que han estado siempre ahí, en el mundo; instalarse en una escucha propiciatoria que saque esas metáforas a la luz. Lorna se asombra de cómo la voz de la naturaleza, por sí sola, hace poesía.

Para Crozier hacer poesía implica sobre todo un tipo peculiar de alerta. Vivir en tal estado de atención es lo que la poeta extraña, según dice, durante los periodos en que por alguna razón deja de escribir. Su concentración no consiste en buscar deliberadamente una metáfora para expresar lo que observa, una parábola eficaz o una sabrosa analogía –"esas cosas vendrán por sí solas", asegura; constituye más bien un estado sosegado de escucha.

Crucial para su quehacer es oír en especial a los animales: al conejo, al ganso, al coyote, al halcón, a la polilla, al perro, a la urraca, al gorrión,

trying out patterns of intonation, entering the zone of sensations created by the flow, welcoming the emotional resonance and recreating the mental space in which the sounds will be heard. For instance, to translate Crozier's poem "Fear of Snakes," I have to plunge into the silent, terrifying "O" that issues from the open jaws of a snake and slithers its way from verse to verse, guiding the poem's development:

> [. . . we]
> watched Larry nail the snake to a telephone pole.
> It twisted on twin points of light, unable to crawl
> out of its pain, its mouth opening, the red
> tongue tasting its own terror, I loved it then,
> that snake. The boys standing there with their stupid hands
> dangling from their wrists, the beautiful green
> mouth opening, a terrible dark O
> no one could hear.

Listening to nature and giving voice to it in the poem

One of Crozier's favorite writers, John Berger, said that poetry "is a question of listening." For Crozier as well, written poetry is neither an invention nor a translation of an intimate vision, but first and foremost a close listening to the world, a listening to the voice of things and creatures. For Lorna, things are only what they are, and in order to write a poem about them, "the things themselves have to speak to me." So it is not a question of mentally manipulating or re-creating them, but of exploring that which animals, phenomena and objects are capable of expressing. Intuitively and devoutly, one has to discover and reveal metaphors that have always existed in the world; listening in such a way as to bring the metaphors to light. Lorna is amazed at how nature voices its own poetry.

For Crozier, writing poetry involves a special alertness above all. It is this living in a state of heightened awareness that she misses during times when, for one reason or another, she is not writing. Her concentration does not involve deliberately seeking out metaphors to express an effective parable or juicy analogy for what she sees; "these things come on their own," she states in what is a sustained state of listening.

Crucial to her work is attentiveness to animals: rabbits, geese, coyotes, hawks, moths, dogs, magpies, sparrows, spiders, groundhogs.

a la araña, a la tuza. A todos ellos se acerca con un amor, más que compasivo, empático. Se reconoce a ella misma en sus actitudes, en su comportamiento, en su presencia. Se siente fascinada por el misterio de todo lenguaje natural.

Ciertamente, mi tarea de traducir a Crozier enfrentó un buen número de dificultades léxicas en lo referente a la fauna y flora, el paisaje y los fenómenos climáticos propios de Canadá, a todo lo cual alude ella con profusión en sus poemas. Se trata, en muchos casos, de especies o fenómenos que no conozco, no sólo por haber vivido siempre en un entorno urbano, sino porque muchos de ellos no se dan en nuestras regiones iberoamericanas y no tienen ni siquiera un nombre de uso común en español.

La voz poética de Lorna Crozier es conversacional, callada, sugerente y, a veces, humorísticamente chispeante. El reto mayor, no sólo como traductora sino como intérprete, fue conservar en español la textura intensamente musical y coloquial que posee su escritura; preservar el efecto paradójico de ternura y humor que tienen muchos de sus poemas y, en fin, ser realmente capaz de evocar el fluir subterráneo de emociones que los recorre. ¿Cómo re-andar, una vez comprendida la significación de los versos, el trayecto que lleva del pensamiento (el contenido, la imagen) a la música primera y natural soñada por la poeta, y de ahí regresar al pensamiento en otra lengua?

Traducir el poema, escuchar su naturaleza propia en uno mismo

Dada mi dificultad para distinguir las armonías sutiles del inglés que aparecen en los versos de Crozier, no he podido sino valerme de mi voz, voz que si no al unísono, al menos en contrapunto dijera sus poemas, habitando aún la atmósfera acústica que generan. Si bien admito que todo poema aguarda la voz silenciosa (íntima) de quien lo lee, cantar en voz alta fue la forma que encontré de dialogar más personalmente con su poesía: Cantarla, primero en inglés, para luego, inmersa en el estado que ese canto me suscitaba, buscar las palabras y giros más justos para devolverla a la escritura en español.

Y es que los poemas de Lorna, siendo canto en primera instancia, provocaron no sólo mi escucha, mi lectura atenta, investigación y reflexión, sino también el ánimo de poner sus versos en mi boca y, como decía el poeta mexicano Jaime Sabines, darles vueltas como a un caramelo. No intenté con ello develar la música secreta de los poemas; más bien "traicionarlos" amistosamente con una nueva musicalidad, que es ya, de suyo, otra "traducción."

She approaches them all with a love born more of empathy than of compassion. She recognizes herself in their attitudes, their behavior, their presence. She is fascinated by the mystery of all natural language.

Of course, while translating Crozier I have come up against numerous lexical difficulties linked to Canada's specific fauna and flora, landscape and climate, all of which she refers to abundantly in her poems. In many cases, the species or phenomena are unknown to me, not just because I have always lived in an urban environment, but also because many of them cannot be found in our Latin-American regions and do not even have a common name in Spanish.

Lorna Crozier's poetic voice is conversational, muted, suggestive and, at times, full of biting humour. The major challenge, not only as a translator but as someone singing her poems, was to retain in Spanish the intensely musical and colloquial texture of her writing; keeping the paradox of gentleness combined with humour found in many of her poems and, most importantly, being truly able to evoke the subterranean flow of emotions. Once I had understood the meaning of the verses, how could I transit from thought (the content or image) to the primary music dreamt by the poet, and from there back to thought in another language?

Translating the poem, listening to the poem's nature in oneself

Given my difficulty distinguishing all the subtle harmonies of English found in Crozier's verses, the best I could do was draw on my own voice to relay her poems, not in unison, but at least as a counterpoint, while still inhabiting the acoustic atmosphere they produced. I acknowledge that every poem awaits the silent (intimate) voice of the reader. Singing out loud, however, was my way of dialoguing more personally with her poetry. By singing her poems in English first and then entering into the state the song created for me, I was able to find the words and turns of phrase I could bring back to Spanish.

Lorna's poems, experienced first as songs, made me not only listen, read attentively, delve further and reflect, they also inspired me to try them out on my tongue and, as Mexican poet Jaime Sabines states, savour them like toffee. The approach is not meant to reveal the secret music of the poems but to find a loving way of "betraying" them with new musicality, in itself another translation.

Si existe un ethos de la traducción poética, creo que éste no tiene que ver tanto con el concepto de "fidelidad" como con el de "consonancia". No puedo ser del todo transparente cuando intento articular en español ideas y cadencias que fueron formuladas originalmente en otra lengua; puedo sólo intentar "sintonizar" con la voz misma del poeta que los creó. Para ello tengo que buscar en mí la tesitura más propicia, propia y a la vez nueva: la voz que yo tendría en caso de decir con la frescura de "la primera vez" los poemas de Crozier. No para re-inventarlos sino para "responder" a ellos, en un diálogo guiado por una profunda afinidad intelectual y empatía. Así pues, "consonancia" significa para mí, como traductora, "cantar junto con el poeta al que traduzco", no al unísono sino en armonía — una extraña armonía entre lenguajes. Ello implica, más allá de la consabida idea expresada en el famoso dicho italiano "traduttore, traditore", la de sumar una segunda voz a la dicción del poema e incluso una segunda línea melódica en contrapunto (contrapunto entre dos musicalidades, dos lenguas y dos modos de hacer poesía); es decir, proponer una nueva musicalidad que se entrelaza con aquella musicalidad originaria del poema, su "contraparte". Para quien lee el poema en su versión traducida, ¿cuál es en realidad la relación entre las líneas que está leyendo y aquellos versos invisibles que las inspiraron? Yo creo que es precisamente una relación de consonancia muy peculiar, como la que se da, por ejemplo, entre la pieza de Bach (que el lector sólo escucha en su memoria) y las líneas del poema de Crozier *The Goldberg Variations* (que el lector tiene ante sus ojos). Tal consonancia no es evidente pero está "ahí" de algún modo – y no sólo debido a las imágenes y conceptos que expresa.

Así también, en las entrelíneas de la versión traducida de un poema reverberan los versos del idioma original. La consonancia se da, pues, entre dos niveles de percepción: la lectura de las líneas negras en la segunda lengua y la audición del silencio sonoro que evocan las blancas entrelíneas – ahí donde respiran invisibles los versos del poema original, como una memoria inconsciente. Ciertamente, en términos poéticos, la virtual armonía entre los versos en dos lenguas distintas no está dada por una mera equivalencia de significados lingüísticos, ni siquiera por un paralelo rítmico o vocálico (imposible de lograr sin detrimento del poema), sino gracias a un espacio de intermediación: el de la imagen y la emoción musical que comparten, emoción previa a cualquier lenguaje verbal, según imagina Lorna Crozier.

Hay algo difícil de explicar, y esto es: la atmósfera musical que comparte un universo de imágenes poéticas en una lengua determinada con el que es posible crear en otra. Y al hablar de "atmósfera musical" no me refiero

If there is a translation ethos where poetry is concerned, I believe it lies not so much in the idea of faithfulness but in that of consonance. I can in no way be transparent when trying to articulate in Spanish ideas and cadences that were originally formulated in another language; all I can do is tune into the very voice of the poet who created the poems. To that end, I have to look inside myself for the best, most fitting and yet new range; the voice I would have were I speaking Crozier's poems with the freshness of a first time. Not to re-invent them but to respond to them in a dialogue guided by deep intellectual affinity and empathy. Thus, to me as a translator, "consonance" means "singing with the poet I am translating," not in unison but in harmony—a strange harmony between languages. It involves, over and above the idea expressed in the famous Italian saying *"traduttore, traditore,"* adding a second voice to the poem's diction and even a second melodic line as counterpoint (between two musicalities, two languages and two ways of creating poetry); in other words, proposing a new musicality that intertwines with the original musicality of the poem, its counterpart. For the person reading the poem in translation, what in fact is the relationship between the lines being read and the invisible verses that inspired them? I believe it is precisely a relationship of special consonance, similar to the one found, for instance, between Bach's piece (which the reader only listens to in memory) and the lines of Crozier's poem "The Goldberg Variations" (which the reader has in front of him or her). The consonance, although not obvious, is "there" in some fashion—not just because of the images and concepts it expresses.

Moreover, between the lines of the translation the verses of the original poem make themselves heard. Hence consonance is between two levels of perception: the reading of the black lines in the second tongue and the sound of the silence evoked by the spaces between the lines—where the invisible verses of the original poem breathe in the unconscious like a memory. Evidently, in poetic terms, the virtual harmony between verses in two different languages does not come about through mere equivalency of linguistic signifiers, or even through a rhythmic or vocal parallel (impossible to attain without doing a disservice to the poem) but through a space for intermediation: that of shared image and musical emotion, an emotion anterior to any verbal language as imagined by Lorna Crozier.

What is difficult to explain is the musical ambience that a universe of poetic images in a given language shares with the universe that can be created in another language. Where I refer to "musical ambience,"

a un género o estilo particular sino a un tempo de dicción, a una intensi-
dad, a un río de sensaciones que nos penetra. Imaginemos a Billie Holiday
cantando versos de Lorna Crozier:

So many write of rain,
its small hands,
the memories it brings,
the sound of things it touches

Con esa misma cadencia y lentitud, con esa deliciosa sensualidad en la voz
(una voz mental), me dispuse a escribir en mi lengua:

Tantos escriben sobre la lluvia,
sus manos breves,
los recuerdos que despierta,
el eco de lo que toca.

Para decir en mi lengua los poemas de Lorna Crozier he debido hacerlo
no sólo con el diccionario y mi competencia lingüística y literaria, sino
empleando todo el cuerpo y la imaginación. Traducirla significa para mí
no un "traslado", sino una interpretación de otra manera de ver el mundo.
He debido escuchar sus poemas en la oquedad de mi conciencia y encontrar luego, dentro de mí, una voz gemela capaz de corear con ella la
experiencia de habitar por un instante ese universo poético que ha creado.
Cantar es una forma de leer un poema con todo el ser de uno, y es sólo mi
"lectura viva" lo que puedo ofrecer. Por contraparte, los versos de Lorna
han prestado a mi voz y a mi escritura nuevas resonancias, nuevas alas y
raíces. Y por ello estoy hondamente agradecida.

"Las infinitas variaciones"

Lorna Crozier dice que la naturaleza hace poesía por sí sola y que el
poema únicamente debe "escuchar" esa poesía primigenia y traducirla al
lenguaje humano. Otros poetas, como Octavio Paz, aseguran que la poesía
se nutre de sí misma, de su tradición, pero es capaz de crear una nueva
naturaleza a partir del lenguaje. Tradición y traición son palabras gemelas.
Los poemas nuevos evocan viejos poemas, los traducen y traicionan a la
vez. La música, anterior quizá a la palabra, guía al poema como una ley
secreta, más profunda que el pensamiento; pero ella también, la música,
responde a una tradición, se nutre de "citas" musicales anteriores, recu-
pera aires antiguos y, traicionándolos, genera nuevas composiciones.

I do not mean a particular genre or style but a tempo in the diction, an intensity, a stream of sensations that penetrates us. Imagine Billie Holliday singing the following verses penned by Lorna Crozier:

> **So many write of rain**
> **its small hands,**
> **the memories it brings,**
> **the sound of things it touches.**

With the same cadence and languor, the delicious sensuality of voice (a mental voice), I prepare to write in my language.

> **Tantos escriben sobre la lluvia,**
> **sus manos breves,**
> **los recuerdos que despierta,**
> **el eco de lo que toca.**

To speak the poems of Lorna Crozier in my language, I have had to use not just a dictionary and my linguistic and literary skills, but my entire body and imagination. Translating is, for me, not just "conveying" but interpreting another way of seeing the world. I had to listen to her poems in the hollow of my consciousness, then find in myself a twin voice capable of composing with her the experience of living briefly in the poetic universe she created. Singing is a way of reading a poem with one's whole being, and my "live reading" is all I have to offer. In exchange, Lorna's verses gave new resonance, wings and roots to my voice and my writing. For this I am deeply grateful.

"Endless variations"

For Lorna Crozier, nature itself makes poetry, and thus a poem need only "listen" and translate it into human language. In the words of other poets such as Octavio Paz, poetry finds nourishment within itself and within its tradition, but is capable of creating yet another nature through language. In Spanish, *tradición* (tradition) and *traición* (betrayal) are twin terms. New poems evoke old poems, while translating and betraying them. Music, which may well predate speech, guides poems like a secret law running deeper than thought; but music also responds to a tradition, is nourished by musical "citations," and resuscitates old tunes only to betray them in order to produce new compositions.

Bach, tan afecto a las fugas, encontraba en las múltiples variaciones de un tópico el impulso de la creación. Cada vez que Gould interpretaba *The Goldberg Variations*, inyectaba a la pieza de Bach un espíritu nuevo. Crozier traduce ese espíritu en un poema personal, para re-interpretar aquella "*music before it became/ the least bit human*". Yo traduzco "las variaciones de Crozier" a otra lengua, donde sus versos encuentran una naturaleza distinta, y luego, poseída por la voz de su poema, canto y me elevo "*like a feathered seed*". Mi versión es, sin duda, una de las posibles infinitas variaciones del poema de Crozier y representa también una "fuga" ("*fugue*": huida).

Vivimos de la poesía como una forma de memoria que regresa y que huye, como una forma de reinterpretar hasta el infinito y darle respiración a la naturaleza que nos habita. La traducción, la traición y la interpretación son, pues, perlas de este collar.

Bach found in multiple variations on a theme his creative impulse, thus his fondness for fugues. Each time Gould interpreted "The Goldberg Variations," he injected Bach's piece with new spirit. Crozier translates that spirit into a personal poem re-interpreting "music before it became/the least bit human." I translate "Crozier's variations" into another language still in which her verses discover another nature. Then, possessed by her poem's voice, I in turn sing and rise up "like a feathered seed." Of course, my version is both one of an infinite number of possible variations on Crozier's poem and a fugue (in Spanish, *fuga* = taking flight).

We live on poetry as on a recurring then fleeing memory and as a way of endlessly re-interpreting and breathing spirit into the nature dwelling in us. Translation, betrayal and interpretation are together pearls of the same necklace.

Translation by S. Ouriou

The Translator's Life:
From Chance to Transcendence

Alexis Levitin

The most important things in life arrive by chance.
But it is up to us to pounce.

I was finishing my Ph.D. in mid-winter and had no idea what to do.
"Any job openings?" I asked the department secretary. "I'll go anywhere!"
She smiled and said "no," but then, smiling again, she reached into a
drawer and pulled out a flyer with the following announcement: "On an
island of lush green rolling hills and spectacular white sand beaches, the
Universidade Federal de Santa Catarina in Florianopolis, Brazil, is seeking
a recent Ph.D. in American Literature to assist in the establishment of a
new graduate level program in English and American Literature
and Language."

I didn't know a word of Portuguese, but I had heard of Pele, the Amazon
River, and Rio de Janeiro. I had also seen *Black Orpheus*. I applied. Three
weeks later, I received a laconic telegram: "Congratulations Stop You have
been chosen Stop" And so I went.

Since my Brazilian graduate students all spoke English, as did my
colleagues, it was in daily life that I began to learn Portuguese. The first
thing I did was to begin reading poetry. Since poetry is a language unto
itself, its inherent austere codes and elliptical byways, with which I already
felt comfortable in English, made it strangely more accessible to me than
ordinary Brazilian prose. I still remember the shocking punch line of the
first Brazilian poem that I read, deciphered, and memorized shortly after
arriving in Florianopolis. The narrator seems to have encountered a kind
of monster on the street, only to discover that "the beast (my God!)
was a man."

Along with poetry, I began to read the daily newspaper. All this was helpful,
of course, but I really only began to speak the language when, after half a
year, I met a lovely and exotic young Brazilian who, luckily for me, could
not speak a word of English. The moment I looked into her enormous
brown eyes, I began to speak Portuguese. A kind of miracle. Or was it
twin-miracles?

The Portuguese language is lovely, but there is no true word for "accomplishment." So, after two and a half years, unable to shake the work ethic of my Americanism, and convinced that I could do nothing to change the happy-go-lucky sensually complacent *tropicalismo* of Brazil, I decided to return to the USA. My best (and richest) student gave me a big carton of books as a good-bye present. When I found myself shuttling between Greenwich Village and the Upper West Side without a job, without a future, with nothing solid to hold on to, I opened my box of Brazilian books and began to read. Finding myself filled with rueful nostalgia for the beautiful country I had chosen to leave, I immersed myself in its language and its images. And of course fell victim to that country's favorite word: *saudades.* The next thing I knew, unable to let go of the beautiful, sonorous language I had learned to love, I was translating. It had begun.

It was 1975. The Latin American literary "boom" was in full sway. For six months, every translation I sent out, whether poetry or fiction, was accepted. I was no one, I had never translated before, yet within a year, in addition to having work in close to a dozen literary magazines, I had published a whole section of Brazilian poetry and prose in *Latin American Literature Today*, a new anthology from Modern Library. Chance had smiled on me. I was translating the right language at exactly the right time. Never having planned to be a translator, I found myself fully launched. Thirty years have passed since then. I've never looked back. I chose my path and it chose me. I am a translator.

Over the years, I came to discover that my personal inclination, my marked preference, was to battle mightily over single images, words, even syllables. I was in love with the problem of translating the music of a language. So I began to drift away from working with fiction and concentrated on poetry. I also drifted away from Brazil and concentrated on Portugal, but not for any significant intellectual or aesthetic reason. Portugal was a small country, easier to handle, easier to visit, more comfortable as a summer vacation destination. It was hard to imagine dragging my one-year-old son to southern Brazil, where in August dead clumps of penguins littered the cold and naked beach. Instead we took him to Portugal, where, before he could even speak, he was running wild across the sands of Sesimbra, a wide-eyed beggar getting plumper and plumper from the generosity of Portuguese families lunching on the beach.

From the beginning, I tried to translate all of the major twentieth century Portuguese poets, but inevitably one must narrow one's focus. And so, after several years, it was clear that two figures attracted me most: Eugénio de Andrade and Sophia de Mello Breyner Andresen. Both shared a love of nature, a love of the sea, and a love of Greece. Both tended toward a classical view, in which all gushing is suppressed and the perfect image or word resonates, surrounded by stillness. Working with these two lovers of the world and the word, I learned to value the importance of every wave and every syllable. And to give the original its due, I had to learn to honor every syllable in my English translation, as well. So, for over a quarter of a century, I devoted much of my time to an attentiveness to sound as the incarnation of beauty in art. Whether this apprenticeship bore splendid fruit or not, I cannot say. I can only say that when I am struggling with a word deep in the night, searching for its echo in English, or in even more straitened circumstances, searching for iambic pentameter rhymed verses in a sonnet, hours pass in which I have utterly forgotten myself in a search for a small touch of beauty. And that unmarked period of time in which I am totally dedicated to the search, that unconscious period of transcendence, is the greatest reward for me as a translator. When you see your name in print months later, it is, of course, a pleasure for your ego, which naturally has returned. But when you are hunting with all your instincts for *le mot juste* at four in the morning, that is the greatest pleasure of all, for you do not exist: you are just an arrow in flight, a mariner steering through the waves toward mythic Ithaca. I hope to keep sailing towards that Ithaca as long as my mind remains intact.

On Translating Aureole
or
The Missing Chapter
or
What It Means to Translate from the Body

Juliana Borrero

> *Translation is the most intimate act of reading.*
> *I surrender to the text when I translate.*
>
> Gayatri Spivak

> *I have needed, I have wanted everything,*
> *perhaps too much.*
>
> Carole Maso

In a place between memory, imagination, experience and the love of language, with an ocean between them, and oceans of words, syntax and blurred vision, two women stand face to face.

"I want to translate you," says the younger one. "I want you to exist in the world of my language."
"You have my blessing," says the one with more experience.

I quiver: excitement, fear. This is a new experience for me, a woman, translating a woman. What will it take to go from me to you?

From my *sur* to your north. My quests to your discoveries. My *trópico* to your winter. My cold feet to your warm blood. An arrangement that may contain all our wild flowers.

I want to translate the world you have shown me; what you have done for me. *Quiero....*

Traducir es tejer, knitting, one needle in each hand, crossing languages, two language actions, writing and translating; now your world and mine. I translate following your track. That was already in me. (Teach me.)

Both women are writers. Both women believe something is chronically wrong with language if there is no room for it to grow, to mutate, to play.

Both women believe literature is exorcism for so much death around us.

Translation, incantation, the transmutation of language from body to body. That strange language process that melts the boundaries of identity between you and me. But not completely.

Translating—already an erotic act—a book about language and desire.

"Between morning and afternoon, sweet apple and rosy pearl, hip and cliff and thighs. Dripping honey, lilting, sweet, Sappho dreams hypnotic sea, waves at her hips, between the lovely legs delirious of a gorgeous nymph" (Maso, *Aureole*, 159).

Women making love to women making love to language making love to…

Shall I whisper to you all of my erotic secrets? Where do we start?

"In the ocean between night and day, word and word, between you and me. The liminal space—between English and French, language and meaning, poetry and prose, in the suspended space between you and me. In the sexual space. In the space between (pink) your breast. In the space (pink) between your mouth (rose) (descending) and my *abricot*. A light fuzz" (Maso, *Aureole*, 25).

Translating a book about all the different forms of exchange, every chapter a different one: sometimes obsessive, violent; sometimes platonic, aching; other times in solitude, delirious, suicidal; or sweet, seductive, playing games with words.

A book about difference, proportion, relation, coming: together and apart. Translating a book that is already about translation.

"Between what I say to you in English and what I say to you in French. In the interval between what is said and the translation."

Translation from skin to skin, from self to other, from one intensity to another, from speaking fluently to barely understanding; between the language and the act, between life and literature, dream and waking, music and poetry, poetry and prose. Only one thing missing: between the writer and translator: the translation process.

"*Aureole* celebrates the resplendence of language and desire. It is a work of reverie and ruin. Pleasure. Oblivion. Joy. A place where we are for a while endlessly possible, capable of anything, it seems: fluid, changing, ephemeral, renewable, intensely alive, close to death, clairvoyant, fearless,

luminous, passionate, strange, even to ourselves" (Maso, *Break Every Rule*, 114).

Translation: to open the space for what does not exist... yet.

I could live in this place. (Stay with me.)

Because life is so different from *Aureole;* and often that difference hurts. The fast rhythms of duty, consumerism, ambition, power, basic out-of-touch-ness.

As if all of life were lived waiting for that rare magic moment of connection, that stoppage of time where suddenly and at last we can listen to ourselves, where something new and real is born in the midst of so much...

There is a promise in the path of your words. I want to hold that place...

I write/translate like someone looking for a path where I will not have to betray myself. Slowly, very slowly recovering the unseen project of a woman's language. A path whose memory is in my body.

It took me centuries to realize what it meant to be a woman. And what that meant with respect to language. The sensation of never fitting anywhere. Blurry images, shapes unseen. None of what we could ever say would ever be close enough...

The discovery of a place...

"We've been waiting a lifetime for you" (Maso, *Aureole*, 201). Unearthing a conversation between so many women, French-speaking, English-speaking Portuguese-speaking, who in turn have worked to unearth...

The invisible suddenly becoming visible... a cave of echoes...

"[desiring bodies of women] yearn, cry out, even 'bleed' for a language of their own making, a language capable of subverting and breaking up both the fictional (discursive) and the real (institutional) order of things" (Gould, 45).

A secret language? A Babbling Tower? A polyphonic underwater teaparty. Call it: *écriture feminine. Écriture au feminin.* Writing from the body.

The first day I read it, I recognized it in the body: the feminine river, the risky edges women jump off of in order to write. I began to trace a pattern, a line of descent, a whole continent unearthed. Virginia Woolf,

Anna Kavan, H.D., Clarice Lispector, Hélène Cixous, Julia Kristeva. Gail Scott, Nicole Brossard, Susanne de Lotbinière-Harwood. The work of Luise Von Flotow, Karen Gould, Suely Rolnick, Deborah Kloepfer. Martha Graham, Dianne Arbus, Camille Claudel. This was just the tip of the iceberg. There was a thinking, a use of language, a form of perception that had simply not been understood in its implications.

"to touch the unity and resonance of our physicality, our bond with the natural order, the corporeal ground of our intelligence" (Adrienne Rich in Gould, 48).

"an epistemological U-turn" (Causse, www.triviavoices.net).

An essential need for promiscuity, the endless reshapings of form.

And nothing was the same again. All the other paths crumbled and I was alone, advancing on this hanging bridge.

My two knitting needles write and translate, write and translate: which one comes first?

To translate from the body it is necessary to understand what the body deeply knows about translation. Always and already. Because language has always and never really been there for us. Because the body has been cut off. Because desire has been cut off. All our strangenesses... Translating all the time.

"I think feminine literature is an organic translated writing... translated from the unknown, like a new way of communicating rather than an already formed language" (Marguerite Duras in Von Flotow, 12).

So I translate you who translate yourself and somewhere in this bleary haze, we meet. In the serious, clinical, drastic love of language. In the hope of a fragmented, sputtered lover's language; the language of the crazy woman or of the seer.

There is a faith in women for new forms of language that will lead to new forms of life:

"If we change language, we change everything" (Warland, 154).

It is here where we meet. Wading through the dark waters of language. Looking for answers. Looking for origin.

"a place where we do not have to apologize" (Maso, *Break Every Rule*, 131).

Because it is also natural for a woman to be tired of translating; all the time explaining. There is the desire to open the window and let all these words out like doves. To know they will go near and far. To think they will be listened to in their own right, their own order, their own logic. Where the act of listening is equivalent to becoming permeable, and blurry vision will have to be reshaped.

To be able to say: language is altered and shaped by the body. It alters and reshapes the bodies that we are.

This makes a difference.

Work with language makes a difference.

"Every translator is an activist" (Brian Mallet, 1998).

Now let's talk about writing, composition, the search for something to hold on to in a young woman writer who has lost all faith in the accepted forms. Who has found the greatest joy in exploration. Sacrificed acceptance for exploring. The girl child having grown strangely in size and intellect.

"I am extremely conscious of the fact that the only space I have is writing. That there is no space for us" (Causse, www.triviavoices.net).

I am interested in composition. How it is that structure holds together. What it is that makes structures different. I am curious about how composition responds to or reconstitutes the structures of a body; how translation becomes a study of composition.

"This work is a novel at the very moment of its forming... the place of all potential. The book is in a state of ravel and unravel to me, forming before our eyes, grouping and regrouping, gathering and dissolving" (Maso, *Break Every Rule*, 125).

In order to translate you I have had to study the light. Its coming and going. Its spectrum of intensities throughout the day.

45 words for radiance. 18 words for turbulence. 23 words for bliss. My chronic indecision. I caress each option like a lover.

I translate your book that is already so much like the translation process. My messy notebooks. My endless collections of words. Loving each moment of the process so much...

12 words for open. 18 words for devastate. 45 words for want.

I learn to translate physically, like jumping on a foot piano. Every phrase a note. I won't change the key.

I learn to read the empty spaces that constitute rhythm.

(Did you know Maya Deren was a dancer before making movies?)

Language so much more than some words on a page...

Incorporate the need for a new language myth, from the body onward. Incorporate all forms of architecture, the intimate shape of the conch, the veins of a celery stalk, the mystery of constellations, algorithms, music, the spaces between words.

Incorporate all the hours and hours of swimming just to feel the deep silence.

As I write this, ten kindergarten pirates with crepe paper bandanas pass my doorstep, on a treasure hunt.

Incorporate the dailiness of life—family reunions, the baby Misha, the beautiful performance artist with the name that means life, the grocery list, forgotten documents in the taxi cab, Linda Perry, the man who jumped from the waterfall and the woman who went to aid him. Moments of compassion, my son growing like a sheath of wheat. The moments of passion, the moments of heartbreak, the falling and falling in love.

As I translate you, a young Colombian gay woman gets a visa to work in San Diego as a tourist bicycle taxi driver. During the day, her thighs get harder as she bears overweight citizens, the lascivious comments of men, over the city hills; on her day off, she goes to the library; during the night she reads *Aureole* to her new American woman friend before making love.

The world is falling from our hands and sometimes all we have is *Aureole*.

That path of light toward...

"One of the greatest pleasures so far has been exploring the sexual energy of the sentence. 'As bleary, delirious the sound of bells, they make their way to the end of the long beach and sentence, far [...] a logic of the body, dramatized by where the line breaks, or the paragraphs, a logic of passion created in the caesuras, in the gaps, where unexpected tensions or emphases'" (Maso, *Break Every Rule*, 121).

In order to translate you I have to trust what I have always wanted. All my rarities—the strangeness of my desire—are a clue down this path.

I trust my syntax to you. I trust that by following closely, adhering to the jumps and claviculae and unfinished business of your syntax, I am—we are—opening a new route in language.

The way the lips begin to open... Opening, opening language.

With no end except joy, no closure except starting and starting, for you, for me, for others who will be there to love, who will be there to read ...

No lilting words for lilting. Nine words for touch. Eleven words for thrill.

I must trust. My internal time. Rhythms violently other than those of the world that is not *Aureole*.

And call for more and more language concentration, language bravery as the translation table becomes a language laboratory and I the measurer, the pourer out of each new formula of desire.

"You can't live here any longer Steven and so you go to spirals light and even motion a circular tower surrounded by water sights and island while on shore you've left a modern Sodom and Gomorrah—you like to think of it" (Maso, *Aureole*, 73).

How far have I gone; how far do I need to go?

If this is real, then translation will have created a place... to remember and return to... whenever we are free enough to revisit the world that is *Aureole*.

This is what I as your translator wish for.

And on desire: is it necessary that I know it all? May I come to you like this, uneven, unfinished? Babbling?

What it means to me... a practical virgin... to translate the work of a lesbian. What does it mean to be a lesbian?

"I mean, really, a lesbian knows what to do with her desire. I could define lesbian as 'Desire.' In the plural: Desires. She is at the origin of a practice which she invents constantly, without any referent, any model" (Causse, www.triviavoices.net).

A lesbian is a woman who precedes women in women's existence. She is an explorer, an anarchist, a feminist who with her body invents everything by force of the attraction she has for other women" (Nicole Brossard, "Kind skin my mind," 43).

This is where the lesbian and the woman meet.

"We are the only possibility for the subject born female to have an ontology. [...] A woman who reappropriates herself becomes either a virgin or a lesbian" (Causse, www.triviavoices.net).

This is what one woman can do for another.

This is where the lover and the translator meet.
Take me to the place of discovery. Teach me what it means to be other. Make me larger than I am. Allow me to make you larger—to introduce a finger, then a hand, then my whole body, under the skin of your text.

I touch. I touch you closer. Lotus. Flower. Your secret.

(I translate from the depths of my secret.)

Unfolding.

17 words for dizzy. 25 words for fall. 32 different ways of saying fuck. So far.

So far.

"The thousand pleasures in this world—*en français*, in English— resplendent, luminous. And dazzle" (Maso, *Aureole*, 11).

...y ahora en español...

May I never finish, may I stay in this light forever. Every new version of this takes a century. It leaves every muscle sore, back aching.

Perhaps I don't want to ever leave the aureole. Making a home here, each time. Childhood refound, I could stay jumping rope forever ...

Translation as a way of staying close... of loving.

From my mountains to your providence.

From your ocean to my subterranean waters.

From my *América* to your America.

From your tongue *a mi lengua...* a kind of kiss.

Translation as a way of continuing.

From what is not seen to what cannot be stopped. From what cannot be understood to what cannot be captured.

The feminine river, the wild track of the feminine in language.

A project of identity.
A project of desire.
A project of language; the 1001 possibilities of form.

... All this is at stake when I knit/translate with my two hands. Such a slow rhythm. *Puntada por puntada.*

I am learning how to feel. Learning if I can trust the thinking that comes from it.

I am using you to reconstitute the texture of my heart.
"Through the urgency and force of my desire and through the open place desire has created in me I may enter my work and be engaged in ways that up until now have been off limits. There is a different engagement—and the stakes begin to make a little bit of sense" (Maso, *Break Every Rule*, 133).

This is what it means to translate from the body.

This is the missing chapter, the pact between translator and writer, two women and language.

Across oceans of language, syntax, blurred vision...

Our hands... touch.

Challenges and Opportunities: Translating Haroldo de Campos's Galáxias

Odile Cisneros

In the universe of the postwar poetic avant-garde in Latin America, the Brazilian poet Haroldo de Campos (1929-2003) commands a place of honor because of his steady commitment to innovation in poetry, criticism, and translation. As early as the mid-1950s, de Campos together with his brother Augusto and their friend Décio Pignatari, began publishing a review they entitled *noigandres*, after a mysterious Provenzal word found in one of the *Cantos* by Ezra Pound (1885-1972), a poet they recognized as their model and mentor. This was the beginning of a poetic movement that became known as "concrete poetry." Concrete poetry was an attempt in Brazil to rescue and update a diversity of historical avant-garde trends by incorporating them into the new vocabularies of advertising, mass media, cybernetics and serial music, among others. The idea was to create mass-oriented poetry. Concrete poetry focused on the materiality of language (sound and visual aspects) and aimed at the instant communication and mass appeal that modern life demanded.

Eventually, concrete poetry gained followers the world over and, to its credit, put Brazil on the global map of the literary avant-garde for the first time. But despite the success of concrete poetry, as early as 1963 de Campos began to devote himself more intensively to other intellectual and poetic pursuits. Besides his growing interest in literary translation, de Campos began to experiment at the time with a new type of writing he termed "*proesia*" (a fusion of poetry and prose), which would culminate in his volume *Galáxias*, completed in 1976 and published in book form for the first time in 1984. *Galáxias* is a book-length prose poem that in many ways is de Campos's response to another of his models, the avant-garde prose of James Joyce (1882-1941) in *Finnegans Wake*, although admittedly not reaching the same radical extremes of Joyce's writing.

Conceived as a series of "fragments" or "formants," each narrating a specific anecdote or travel incident (some real, some purely linguistic), *Galáxias* charts the literal and literary journeys de Campos undertook from the early 1950s on. The title alludes to the peculiar way in which the text unfolds as an ever-expanding galaxy, where the initial word of each of the fifty parts of the poem contains, so to speak, the origin of all others.

The text also relies on a number of poetic devices that produce its specific texture and present a number of challenges and opportunities for the translator. I will discuss seven of these devices and the solutions sought in the translation.

The challenges that *Galáxias* presents to the reader, let alone the translator, are not insignificant nor easily met, however, they are also not insurmountable. As de Campos himself argued in a key text on translation he authored in 1963—the same year he began writing *Galáxias*—the "impossibility" of translating a literary text where form and content are inseparable does not necessarily lead to the abandonment of the task. Instead, the corollary he derives from this apparent impasse is the necessity to recreate the forms, to produce an autonomous yet parallel creation that maintains an isomorphic relation to its "original." De Campos stresses this "autonomy" of translation while at the same time bringing out the isomorphism between translation and original:

> The [two] texts [namely, original and translation] may exist [...] in two languages and as two bodies of autonomous aesthetic information, which, we should like to add, will be linked to each other through an isomorphic relation: they will be different in language, but like isomorphic bodies, they will crystallize within the same system (Campos, "Translation as Creation and Criticism" 315).

In a way, the theory put forth is interdependent on the choice of texts to be translated, it is intimately connected to that choice because the nature of those texts calls for this sort of "creative" translation.

Interestingly, the program of writing that de Campos promoted was also isomorphically linked to his ideas on translation. In other words, the texts de Campos produced demand the type of translation he advocated, and that specific practice of translation in turn had a major impact on his own writing practices. In this way, the translations he produced of texts by James Joyce, Ezra Pound, Stéphane Mallarmé, Chinese classical poetry and Russian futurist poetry, to mention just a few examples, might very well be considered creations parallel to their originals that also influenced his own writing practice. This too inspired my own method when translating de Campos's masterpiece *Galáxias* in collaboration with the renowned translator of the Hispanic literary avant-garde Suzanne Jill Levine (a task made possible to a large extent by the BILTC residency). We attempted to identify the challenges and devices at play in *Galáxias* and "transcreate," to use de Campos's own terminology, rather than just translate. As it will become

obvious in the discussion below, the solutions we found to some of the challenges were "creative" with an eye to replicating the forms and patterns and at times deviating considerably from the strict semantic content of the text.

Perhaps the first, most obvious challenge when trying to produce "parallel creation" for any piece of poetry is, as Eliot Weinberger, Octavio Paz's celebrated translator, put it "to invent a new music for the text in the translation-language, one that is mandated by the original. A music that is not a technical replication of the original" (111). This is particularly true of *Galáxias*, a text in which the sound and oral aspects are so prominent. *Galáxias*'s play with sound goes back to de Campos's initial experiments with concrete poetry. Earlier I mentioned the emphasis that concrete poetry had placed on the material aspects of language (visual and sound). However, despite the "verbi-voco-visual" program that concrete poetry laid out, and despite certain experiments with sound, one could safely argue that sonic play nevertheless played second fiddle to visual form in most concrete poetry initially. So much so that, for years, "concrete poetry," at least in Brazil, was almost synonymous with "visual poetry" and there was no real equivalent to "sound poetry" in the sense of the Dada performances by figures such as Hugo Ball and Kurt Schwitters. Eventually, though, the visual play was for the most part abandoned by Haroldo de Campos in favor of sound. This is evident in *Galáxias*, which, while still retaining some basic visual elements—such as the layout of the poem printed only on one side of the page—emphasized sound instead, becoming the closest thing to "sound poetry" in Haroldo de Campos's production. Translating the sound then is an enormous challenge that involved recognizing the rhythmic patterns, the puns, alliterations, internal and vocalic rhymes and producing a parallel pattern, a music that could echo the effects of the original.

A fundamental difference between the syllabic structures of English and Portuguese makes this particularly tricky: in Portuguese, most syllables have the same length or duration and most words are paroxytonic, contrasting with the monosyllabic patterns of English and its irregularity in stress. Here the choice was to translate the slower, more andante rhythm of Portuguese by the monosyllabic staccato of English and a transposition of the stresses. In this way, the initial words of the first formant of *Galáxias*, *"e começo aqui e meço aqui este começo e recomeço e remeço e arremesso e aqui me meço quando se vive sob a espécie da viagem o que importa não é a viagem mas o começo,"* becomes the more economic "and here I begin I spin here the beguine I respin and begin to release and realize life begins." The original

makes use of a number of end-rhymes in "*eço*." In this translation by Suzanne Jill Levine, the translator chose to incorporate the pun in Cole Porter's song "Begin the Beguine" in the spirit of play with references to popular culture elsewhere in de Campos's text. ("Begin" also—and this may be obvious—is an explicit reference to Genesis "in the beginning," since this initial formant of the poem not only opens the entire series of prose poems but also thematically deals with beginnings.) "Begin," rhymes with "spin" in the sense of weaving, weaving a text, a story, and then "release" "realize life," where the translator switched from end-rhymes to alliteration. In English this is normally considered an unsophisticated literary device, yet it has a venerable history and affiliation with some of the earliest poetic texts of the Anglo-Saxon tradition such as the epic poem *Beowulf* and the elegiac poem *The Seafarer*, in Ezra Pound's translation:

> **"The Seafarer"**
> **May I for my own self song's truth reckon,**
> **Journey's jargon, how I in harsh days**
> **Hardship endured oft.**
> **Bitter breast-cares have I abided,**
> **Known on my keel many a care's hold,**
> **And dire sea-surge, and there I oft spent**
> **Narrow nightwatch nigh the ship's head**
> **While she tossed close to cliffs (Pound 207).**

Although, in English, the use (and abuse) of alliteration is not considered to be "in good taste," from the point of view of the baroque-izing aesthetics of *Galáxias* which plays with the limits of such notions and even deliberately approaches kitsch, I believe the choice, on account of the sound play, was justified.

Sound has a direct relationship to the author's conception of *Galáxias* as a performative text. As de Campos declares in the notes to the final (posthumous) edition, "it is a book that was meant to be read out loud, which proposes a rhythm and a prosody, whose 'obscure' passages become transparent when read aloud and whose words, when orally performed, can acquire a talismanic force, can soothe and seduce, like a mantra" (Campos, *Galáxias*, n.p.). This oral aspect of the text has to be taken into account in the choices made when translating. A case in point is the fragment "*circuladô de fulô*," also one of the most difficult ones to translate. This fragment relates de Campos's visit to a country fair in northeastern Brazil where he

reportedly heard an itinerant musician playing an instrument made from a wire, a stick and a gourd (something like a capoeira berimbau) and singing a song with the words "*circuladô de fulô.*" The word "*circuladô*" is an oral form of the word "*circulador*," a turning mechanism such as a fan, and "*fulô,*" a vernacular form of "*flor*" (flower) used particularly in the Northeast of Brazil, as in the famous popular song "*Pisa na Fulô.*" Another possible meaning of the word "*circuladô*" that de Campos points out in his notes to the fragment is "surrounded" or "encircled." In my first attempts at translating this fragment, I tried to come up with a phrase that privileged the mysterious semantics of this phrase, both as something (or someone) surrounded by flowers or a circular force that is somehow also connected to flowers. I used the invented phrase "flower-gyre," inspired by the Lewis Carroll's nonsense poem "Jabberwocky":

> `Twas brillig, and the slithy toves
> Did gyre and gimble in the wabe:
> All mimsy were the borogoves,
> And the mome raths outgrabe.

Although I liked the sound and the allusion, I soon realized that rhythmically "flower-gyre" did not work very well when read out loud and lost the mysterious polysemy of the original word. I then decided to switch to a play on words that would include a reference to flowers, to a boundary and to the action of a fan (the implicit image is also that the round shape of a fan and its blades is mirrored in the shape of a flower, as it appears on the cover of the record "*Circuladô*" by the popular Brazilian musician and lyricist Caetano Veloso, who set part of the fragment to music). The phrase then became "Flower-border flower-blow," with the following variations in the course of the fragment: "flower-blower flower-flow" "flower-border flower-blow flower-border flower blow flower-border flower-blo." This second solution maintains a rhythm similar to that of the original and has the same number of syllables.

"*Circuladô de fulô*" also exemplifies another recurrent feature of the text that becomes an issue for the translator, namely, the coexistence and constant change in linguistic registers, what linguists call "code-switching." In my conversations regarding this fragment with Ivan de Campos, the poet's son, I understood that two registers coincide in this mysterious phrase: the popularizing one (as I've noted above regarding the vernacular use of this word) and a poetic and erudite one ("a force that causes circulation"). It is important to understand these deviations where de

Campos mixes popular forms of speech, slang and even vulgar language with erudite expressions and deliberately bookish and archaic language.

Everything converges toward a sort of catalogue of the Portuguese language, much in the same way that Joyce's *Ulysses* does (as K. David Jackson has noted), and also, once more, like *Finnegans Wake*, where erudite verbal games mingle with puns and vulgarisms. The result of this mix of registers in the translation, as Joan Lindgren, a fellow translator commented, is that it becomes a kind of "rap for intellectuals." I'm certain the popular urban poetics of rap were in the back of my mind—albeit not consciously—as I tried to replicate the sounds, rhythms and "popular" registers of *Galáxias* in this translation.

Despite these incursions into the popular, there is still much that is erudite and "cultured" in *Galáxias*, and not just in the use of certain words, where de Campos resorts to the first, and already obsolete, meaning of a word. Some passages of the text display what the French philosopher, Jacques Derrida, in a public homage to de Campos in 1996, called de Campos's "absolute, atemporal, definitive, inalterable, indubitable knowledge." This presupposes a familiarity with his work and the work of the poets de Campos studied, translated and promoted. For instance, when de Campos speaks of "*o velho poeta comendo as pedras da vitória*," it would be easy to mindlessly translate this as "the old poet eating the stones of victory," assuming perhaps a strangely festive allusion to Carlos Drummond de Andrade and João Cabral de Melo Neto, two celebrated modernist poets of Brazil whose poems refer recurrently to stones. Those allusions could be there, but without a doubt here de Campos is specifically and metaphorically referring to Joaquim de Sousândrade, the late Romantic Brazilian poet, author of a 300-page trans-American epic poem entitled *Guesa Errante* [Wandering Guesa], whose work de Campos and his brother Augusto admired and republished in the early 1960s, rescuing him from oblivion. According to biographical information, after traveling the world over, living in Europe and in New York, Sousândrade, a Greek and Latin scholar by training, returned in a state of dire poverty to Quinta da Vitória, his estate in the Northeast of Brazil, which he allegedly began to sell, stone by stone, in order to survive. The "*pedras da vitória*" are, thus, literally, the stones of his landed estate. And so on, with countless references throughout *Galáxias*.

Another aspect of de Campos's erudition displayed in *Galáxias* has to do with the inclusion of numerous foreign words and phrases throughout the text in Portuguese. English, French, German, Spanish, Italian, ancient Greek, Latin, and if we count proper nouns and place names, Hindi, Náhuatl, Basque, Chinese, Japanese, Arabic, Russian and Czech literally become con-fused in this "Babelian" text. I don't believe this is merely a pedantic show of linguistic sophistication: even for the author himself, despite his linguistic flair, the words in other languages (particularly the more obscure ones) represent an experience of the foreign and are included for their "mantric value." As de Campos explains: "Regarding the words and phrases in other languages—always carrying a mantric, 'transmental,' value even when not always apprehensible on a semantic level—those words and phrases are usually translated or glossed in the context, in this way flowing along and into the rhythm of the whole" (*Galáxias* n.p.). These introjected fragments, besides being *objets trouvés* in this textual collage with an important referential function, more importantly perform a material function of sound estrangement.

What to do about those words, the translator could ask herself, especially when confronted with an English-language public who would be less than multilingual, perhaps even, monolingual? For instance, in the fragment "*reza calla y trabaja*," this phrase, a political slogan that evokes Franco's Spain, is repeated constantly in Spanish in the original without a translation. In the translation, we decided to alternate the phrase in Spanish with a version into English instead of using the Spanish constantly. Although this is not what de Campos does in the original—because for a Brazilian reader the Spanish of the phrase is almost transparent—he does do that in the case of languages that would be less familiar to the Brazilian public. In certain cases, though, we maintained the foreignness of the "foreign" language as well as the strangeness of the passages that appear in English in the original. This, in a sense, is what some translation scholars call deliberately "foreignizing" as opposed to domesticating translation strategies.

Another challenge in this translation had to do with the syntactic differences between Portuguese and English, particularly because the text lacks any punctuation or capitalization. The freer syntax of Portuguese presents a problem, especially because English has a much more rigid word order structure. Adjectives, for instance, usually follow the noun in Portuguese, but can be inverted for effect. In English, putting the adjective after the

noun creates an affected diction, but interestingly also produces on occasion semantic ambiguity, since the adjective may be modifying the preceding or the subsequent noun.

In this same vein, another interesting feature of *Galáxias*, and the last of the challenges I will discuss here, is the poetic device known as enjambment, which continues a syntactic unit from one line of a poem to the next without pause. In this particular case there were occasions where some of these enjambments could not be maintained, but to compensate I tried to exaggerate or maintain others in order to produce greater ambiguity, surprise, and even humor. I believe this is a point that escaped other translators who saw *Galáxias* as a kind of uninterrupted prose. This is reflected in the way the translations were printed, that is, without attention to the ends of the lines, which in my opinion are crucial. De Campos himself refers to the more than 2000 "*versículos*" of the work. "*Versículos*" is a Portuguese word used to refer specifically to verses in the Bible, but it of course maintains an etymological relationship with "*verso*," as in line of "verse," and the act of keeping the enjambment and attention to the ends of the lines allows the reader to produce a dynamic oralization of the text in English.

In conclusion, it is worth noting that, as with de Campos's own translation practice in his radical translations of classical and avant-garde texts, the challenges that the complexity of *Galáxias* presents to the translator in turn effectively sanction opportunity for creative translation.

Traducción de poesía: ¿misión imposible o cuestión de maña?

Françoise Roy

La poesía es, según se dice, la crema y nata de la literatura. En boca del protagonista de la novela *Disgrace*, de J.M. Coetzee, la poesía funciona como el relámpago, es amor a primera vista. O como dice este encumbrado autor sudafricano en otro de sus libros, que recoge sus presuntas memorias narradas en tercera persona, el trabajo del poeta consiste en exprimir las piedras hasta sacarles sangre. Si bien es cierto que de todos los escritores, los más conscientes del peso y del lugar de las palabras son los poetas, el aura de misterio que ha rodeado la poesía hasta nuestros días ha dado lugar a una idea peregrina: que es casi imposible traducir poesía. Al menos, se afirma a diestra y siniestra que la poesía pierde mucho al ser traducida, y se evocan conceptos tan nebulosos como el "espíritu" de un libro. De la misma manera, los islamistas más ortodoxos alegan que el Corán es intraducible, que sólo puede recitarse, escribirse y leerse en árabe pese a que el Islam predomina en países con lenguas tan diversas (como el turco, el albanés, el kurdo, el farsi, urdu, hindi, bengalí, afgano, malayo, tailandés o indonesio). Lo mismo sucede con la poesía que, de acuerdo con los griegos, era obra de misteriosas musas que insuflaban en la pluma del poeta algo emparentado, incluso etimológicamente, con el soplo. Algo que en otras nomenclaturas se ha llamado "numen", "duende" o "inspiración". Tal vez de ahí surgió la idea —que he oído mencionar más de una vez, e incluso recientemente de boca de un académico— de que no se puede traducir poesía. Si bien es cierto que en la balanza estética el texto narrativo privilegia el sentido sobre la forma, mientras que el poema privilegia el sonido (es decir, la forma) por encima del sentido, creo que sostener que la poesía es intraducible o que se demerita mucho al ser traducida deriva de una visión radical de ella como algo que fuese sólo sonido (o forma, dicho de otra manera).

No abordaré aquí el hecho de que la poesía, en efecto, no está obligada a ceñirse al mismo grado de coherencia que la prosa narrativa. Sin embargo, esto no implica que no pase de ser un experimento lingüístico que se resume a mera forma. Detrás de esa forma, que sigue siendo la camisa de fuerza del poema a pesar de que la modernidad nos ha liberado del yugo de la métrica tradicional y de la rima, hay, siempre, un sentido. Por ende, el problema, para el traductor no es plasmar una metáfora o una imagen, más o menos acertadamente en otro idioma, pues el puro sentido

Poetry Translation:
Mission Impossible or a Question of Skill?

Françoise Roy

They say that poetry is the *nec plus ultra* of all literature. In the words of J.M. Coetzee's protagonist in his novel *Disgrace*, poetry is like lightning or falling in love. Or as the eminent South African author states in another work from his semi-autobiographical series written in the third person, a poet's work involves squeezing blood from stones. It is true that poets, more than any other writer, are most fully aware of the weight and place of words, yet the aura of mystery that has always surrounded poetry has given rise to the peculiar idea that it is next to impossible to translate poetry. Or, at the very least, it is widely held that poetry loses a great deal in translation; here concepts as nebulous as the "spirit" of a book are invoked. Similarly, the most orthodox Islamists allege that the Koran is untranslatable, that it can only be recited, written and read in Arabic despite the importance of Islam in many countries where other languages are spoken (such as Turkish, Albanese, Kurd, Farsi, Urdu, Hindi, Bengali, Afghan, Alaysian, Thai and Indonesian). The same occurs with poetry, which the Greeks believed was the result of mysterious muses infusing a poet's pen with something akin—even etymologically—to the breath, or what other nomenclatures have referred to as "*numen*," "*duende*," or "inspiration." Perhaps this explains the claim—that I have heard on more than one occasion and even recently by an academic—that poetry is untranslatable. In the aesthetic balance, prose gives precedence to meaning over form and poetry gives precedence to sound (in other words, form) over meaning, however, I believe that the argument that poetry is untranslatable or loses immeasurably in translation stems from a radical vision of poetry as something that relies on sound (or, put differently, on form) alone.

I will not dwell on the fact that poetry, indeed, is not required to meet the same level of coherence as narrative prose. However, this does not mean that poetry is nothing but a linguistic experiment easily summarized as pure form. Behind form—which continues to be the poem's straitjacket even if the modern era has dispensed with the yoke of traditional metrics and rhyme—meaning can always be found. Hence the problem for translators is not that of coming up with a different metaphor or image since the pure meaning of language will inevitably take care of that aspect

del lenguaje se va a encargar de ello. Si un verso dice "*pavillon en viande saignante*", como versa una famosa línea del hasta nuestros días insuperable Arthur Rimbaud, eso mismo quiere decir en otro idioma, entendamos o no qué representa o simboliza ese pabellón: sólo Rimbaud, si aún estuviese vivo, podría decírnoslo más allá de cualquier duda razonable. Cierto grado de hermetismo semántico es imprescindible en un poema; de no ser así, no hay poesía.

El reto de quien traduce poesía del español al francés es el mismo que el de todo aquel que traduce poesía desde cualquier idioma hacia cualquier otro idioma: reproducir el sentido con sonidos que no resulten cacofónicos, que jueguen con el ritmo, que resulten en una sonoridad atractiva en la lengua meta. No será igual, pues cada idioma tiene su propia melodía, pero no dejará de ser sonoridad de todos modos.

Ahora bien, si nos concentramos en la traducción del español al francés, tendremos que atender dificultades adicionales que tienen que ver con la estructura de la lengua de meta y que todo traductor de poesía del español al francés conoce de sobra: la abundancia de monosílabos en francés, que tienden a acortar o atropellar los versos quitándoles musicalidad; la aparente guturalidad del francés, que si uno excluye la jota en español, siempre plantea retos de sonoridad muy particulares. El "exceso" de artículos y pronombres personales, así como la existencia del artículo partitivo y la obligación de usar sujeto dicho e inequívoco siempre, se suman a tales dificultades. La lista de escollos es larga, como lo es cualquier lista de problemas cuando uno debe trasladar un sentido y una forma de un idioma a otro, cualesquiera que estos sean. Y ello —por ejemplo, la presencia obligada de pronombres personales antes del verbo en francés— nos devuelve a la cuestión del sentido que abordé antes, y específicamente, a una característica intrínseca del idioma galo frente al castellano: el francés, y aquí voy a destrozar su reputación de lengua romántica y fluida, es una lengua sumamente precisa. Mucho más que el inglés, que sin embargo tiene fama de ser exacto y frío. El francés es tan preciso, tan quirúrgico, tan poco flexible, que casi nunca se puede cambiar el orden de las palabras en una frase. Es un idioma en el que no ha habido cambios ortográficos en siglos, y cuya estricta sintaxis deja poco margen para la creatividad. La casi inalterabilidad del orden léxico es el mayor reto de musicalidad y belleza cuando uno traduce versos al francés; si bien en español uno puede evitar fácilmente una gran cantidad de rimas indeseables al mover las palabras de lugar, en francés, esto no es posible. Al menos, casi nunca. En francés, es necesario recurrir a otros trucos que la mera posición de las palabras para eliminar ciertas rimas indeseables —ya sean asonancias o rimas más tradicionales—,

in another language. If a verse speaks of "*le pavillon en viande saignante*," as in the famous line from the incomparable Arthur Rimbaud, it means the same thing in another language, whether or not we know what the pavilion represents or symbolizes: only Rimbaud, if he were still alive, could banish all doubt; a certain level of hermetism in semantics is unavoidable in a poem; if not, there would be no poetry.

The challenge for translators of poetry from Spanish to French is the same for any translator of poetry irrespective of the languages involved: reproducing meaning with non-cacophonous sounds that play with rhythm and lead to an engaging sonority in the target language. There will be differences since each language has its own melody, but sonority will still be found.

Now, if we focus on translation from Spanish into French, we have to expect additional difficulties linked to the target language's structure, one that translators from Spanish to French are all too familiar with: the abundance of monosyllables in French that tend to shorten or disrupt verses and affect their musicality; and the perceived gutturality of French that represents a particular challenge where sound is concerned (the only guttural sound in Spanish being the "j"). The "excessive" number of articles and personal pronouns as well as the use of the *partitif* [*du, de la, des*] and the requirement to always use an unequivocally stated subject only increase the difficulty. The list of pitfalls is long, as is any list of problems when meaning and form must be translated from one language into another, whatever the language. The mandatory presence of personal pronouns before a verb in French, for instance, brings us back to the question of meaning broached earlier on, and more specifically, to an intrinsec characteristic of the French as opposed to the Spanish—here I will destroy the former's reputation as a flowing, romantic language—that is, its level of precision. French is much more precise than English, which itself is widely considered to be exact and cold. French is so precise, so clinical and so inflexible that the order of words in a sentence can rarely be modified. It is a language that has not undergone changes in spelling for centuries, and whose strict syntax leaves little leeway for creativity. For the translator, its virtually unalterable lexical order is the main challenge to musicality and beauty. In Spanish, a large number of undesirable rhymes can be avoided by changing the position of words; in French, this is impossible. Or next to impossible. In French, techniques other than the mere position of words must be employed to eliminate both unwanted rhyme—more traditional assonance or rhyming—and a whole host of cacophonic combinations.

sin contar un sinfín de combinaciones cacofónicas: hay que transformar los adjetivos en sustantivos y viceversa; hay que añadir ripios (es decir, en jerga poética, rellenos que no modifican el sentido de la oración); hay que buscar (a veces, desesperadamente) sinónimos e ideas afines. Sin embargo, para hacer uso de esos trucos lingüísticos —ripios, sinónimos, cambios de lugar en el orden de las palabras—, hay que atender primero algo más urgente: saber exactamente qué quiso decir el poeta. En prosa es relativamente fácil de elucidar; en poesía, no. Si bien he dicho que los sentidos se mantienen aun en poesía, aun en versos muy herméticos y extremadamente polisémicos (pienso en la poesía de Lezama Lima, por ejemplo), debo subrayar aquí que lo que constituye uno de los mayores arcanos de la poesía actual es justamente su "incomunicabilidad". Dice el poeta uruguayo Eduardo Milán que, lejos de ser un defecto de la poesía moderna, la incomunicabilidad —es decir, el hecho de que un lector nunca esté seguro de lo que quiere decir el poeta— es una virtud de la poesía moderna. Lo que, hace menos de dos siglos —a saber, la falta de claridad—, era considerado seña de malos versos se ha vuelto hoy en día un valor agregado. La poesía es, en esencia, polisémica, y puede serlo hasta llegar a lo incomunicable. En un poema, uno se puede contradecir y es válido decir algo cuyo significado sólo sabría descifrar el poeta mismo; la multiplicidad de sentidos posibles, de interpretaciones potenciales, deviene riqueza y no detrimento. El español se presta muy bien a esa operación de polisemia por ciertas características estructurales que posee: la frecuente y permitida ausencia de sujeto nombrado puede enriquecer un poema porque deja al lector varias opciones de sujetos posibles, a veces intercambiables incluso, y esa ambigüedad es a menudo buscada y deliberada. En francés, uno no se puede dar tal lujo.

Los verbos en la narrativa castellana también pueden prescindir de sujetos explícitos, pero éstos últimos están dados por el contexto. En poesía, la obligación lingüística de aludir, aunque sea por el puro contexto, a la identidad del sujeto no existe como tal, y el poeta se vale de ello para ser ambiguo cuando así lo desea. Sobran ejemplos de ambigüedad, y son tan claros en español que resultan casi caricaturescos: si un verso, por ejemplo, dice "sus hermanos" en español, el traductor al francés debe conocer a ciencia cierta el género de esos hermanos, y saber además si hay más de uno en cada sexo, para poder decidir si debe traducir la frase como "ses frères", "leurs frères", "ses frères et sa soeur", "son frère et sa soeur", "ses frères et ses soeurs", "son frère et ses soeurs", "leurs frères et leur soeur", "leurs frères et leurs soeurs", "leur frère et leur soeur", "leur frère et leurs soeurs". Lo mismo sucede con la palabra "sueño", que aparece muy seguido en los versos porque la materia misma de un poema está íntimamente

Adjectives must be changed to substantives and vice versa; padding must be added (or fillers, as they're called, that don't change the meaning of the poem). One must look for (at times desperately) synonyms or like concepts. However, something more urgent must be addressed before linguistic techniques—fillers, synonyms and changes in word order—can be used: what exactly did the poet mean? The answer is easy enough with prose, less so with poetry. Despite my claim that meaning still exists in poetry, even in hermetic, extremely polysemic verses (I'm thinking of Lezama Lima's work, for example), I must point out that one of the arcana of contemporary poetry is in fact its "incommunicability." According to Uruguayan poet Eduardo Milán, far from being a flaw, the incommunicability of modern poetry—that is, the fact that a reader can never be absolutely sure of the poet's meaning—is seen as a virtue. That which less than two centuries ago was considered a sign of bad poetry—lack of clarity—has become a strength in today's world. Poetry is by its very essence polysemic, even to the point of incommunicability. A poem may contain contradictions, a poet is entitled to say things that only he or she can decipher; and the multiplicity of meanings and interpretations is seen as an advantage not a drawback. Spanish suits polysemic operations because of certain structural characteristics: the frequent and permissible absence of a named subject enriches poems since readers are given several, sometimes interchangeable, options; ambiguity is often intentional and deliberate. French does not offer the same luxury.

Verbs in Spanish prose don't require explicit subjects either, however, the latter are provided by the context. In poetry, there is no linguistic obligation to allude to a subject's identity, not even through context, and the poet is able to play with that freedom and remain ambiguous where desired. There are many examples of ambiguity, some so obvious in Spanish as to border on caricatures. For instance, if a verse reads *sus hermanos* in Spanish, the translator into French must know the gender of the *hermanos* and whether there is more than one of each gender in order to decide whether to use *ses frères, leurs frères, ses frères et sa soeur, son frère et sa soeur, ses frères et ses soeurs, son frère et ses soeurs, leurs frères et leur soeur, leurs frères et leurs soeurs, leur frère et leur soeur* or *leur frère et leurs soeurs*. The same can be said of the word *sueño*, a term often found in verse since the stuff of poetry itself is intimately tied to the oniric. Except in instances where the context is self-explanatory, more often than not the word poses a problem: is this *sommeil* (the sleeping state) or *rêve* or even *songe* (what is dreamt)? An *escalera* can be referred to as *escalier* or *échelle* in French, depending on whether or not it can be moved. Let's not forget the possessive *su* from my first example,

ligada a lo onírico. Con la salvedad de los casos en los que el contexto habla por sí solo, esta palabra casi siempre representa un problema: se tratará de "sommeil" (el estado de no vigilia) o de "rêve", si no es que de "songe" (lo que se sueña). Una escalera en francés se puede decir "escalier" o "échelle", dependiendo de su capacidad o incapacidad de moverse. Ni hablar, desde luego, del posesivo "su", que acabamos de mencionar en el primer ejemplo; en español, no nos informa sobre la identidad del poseedor (es decir, no nos dice si se trata de una o más personas, y si éstas son hombres o mujeres). Si bien en francés, en cambio, el posesivo no nos dice quién es el poseedor, el resto de la frase nos lo dice sin falta porque todo verbo conjugado necesita sujeto explícito. Y de pilón, el posesivo en francés nos da información sobre el número y género del objeto poseído. Huelga decir que la lista de escollos de este tipo se alargaría cual rollo del Mar Muerto, pues el castellano está plagado de ambigüedades que lo hacen rico y relativamente poco preciso.

En resumidas cuentas, el verdadero reto de un traductor de poesía del español al francés no es tanto trasladar imágenes de una lengua a otra como creen los legos en la materia, sino pasar de la riqueza y ambigüedad característica del español a la precisión en filigrana del francés, teniendo en mente que en poesía, la forma es tan importante como el fondo.

which in Spanish provides no information on the person's identity (whether it refers to one person or more, whether the person is male or female). In French, the possessive doesn't give us the identity of the person in question, however, the rest of the sentence inevitably does just that since any conjugated verb requires an explicit subject. The French possessive also gives us the gender and number of the possessed object. It should be stated that a list of similar difficulties would be as long as the Dead Sea scroll since Spanish is plagued with ambiguity, making it both rich and relatively imprecise.

In summary, the true challenge for a translator of poetry from Spanish to French is not, as those unversed in the field might think, the translation of images from one language to another, but the passage from the rich ambiguity characteristic of Spanish to the filigreed precision of French, keeping in mind all the while that, where poetry is concerned, form is as important as content.

Translation by S. Ouriou

The World of Translation

bey
en
d wo
rds

Translating
the World

The Subversive Scribe

Suzanne Jill Levine

Subversion and modernity were terms often uttered in
the same breath: part of what made art modern was its capacity to shock.
But by the 1970s, with post-modernity in full swing, the aesthetics that
used to *épater la bourgeoisie* became a new aesthetics for whatever sectors of
society were still genuinely engaged with the arts. The writers featured in
my book—Guillermo Cabrera Infante, Manuel Puig and Severo Sarduy—
came of literary age in the postmodern era, and I began translating them
on the eve of the '70s. By this time the word "subversion" had acquired
an ironic fringe.

The Subversive Scribe, which was first going to be called "The Invisible
Scribe," is at least two books in one: a translator's journal and literary
criticism. Unfolding under general headings designating what are conven-
tionally called the "problems" of translation, the chapters lead the reader
to the writers as well as to the cultures which begat both originals and
translations. The goal: make the translator's presence (traditionally invisible) visible and comprehensible. Who is the translator? scholar, linguist,
trickster, traitor, conqueror, slave, or simply, as Gregory Rabassa has inti-
mated, a timid writer? The translator can be all these personae, but she
or he must be a writer.

The translator in my study is a collaborator rather than "handmaiden,"
the latter being one of tradition's misogynist labels for this oft maligned
but indispensable figure in literary history. My collaborators in the projects
explored in this book were the authors of the original works. Because the
translator is the protagonist of my book, the scribe was no longer invisible, so a friend at the time suggested the transformation from invisible to
subversive. The title's irony was to pass beneath the radar of some of the
book's readers—which is why I would like to take the opportunity of this
new preface to underscore the point.

While its ideological or political sense is certainly implied, subversion, a
battle cry in the mid-sixties, was meant mostly to send up the tread-worn
categories of "fidelity" and "betrayal," to provoke or invite readers to
rethink what translation is: a creative mode of writing in which the translator takes on the voice of a foreign writer. If translations are betrayals

à la *traduttore traditore*, why not think of them as deliberate betrayals, that is, subversions? Subversion "betrays" in the sense of exposing those theories seeking to pigeonhole, to impose categories such as "untranslatable" and to limit the creative writer's journey, theories that censor the contradictions played out in the literary arts.

The Subversive Scribe is about creative collaboration with and between writers and about how writers perceive writing. Translating alongside the author or with a learned native speaker was the surest way to approach the original as closely as linguistically possible, and as a translator I had the good fortune to work with some of the most gifted literary artists of their time, the Latin American "boom" era of the sixties and seventies. Writers like Puig and Cabrera Infante pushed the novel toward a post-modern aesthetic without losing the reader's engagement, and the process of translation was for them an integral part of the creative process.

The three writers I focus on here were all Latin Americans in exile; each in his own way was a subversive, and not only as literary artist. Subversion means to most of us political subversion, like terrorism or, in the old days, revolution. Guillermo Cabrera Infante, who started out as a Cuban revolutionary, would confront Castro's censorship campaigns in the 1960s at a time when such an attitude was unfashionable and even dangerous for an intellectual. His books are still not circulated officially in today's Cuba. Severo Sarduy, a Cuban who did not return to his country to avoid being interned in a work camp for homosexuals, considered himself Maoist *à la française*. The Argentine Manuel Puig was a "queer" who dared to explore sexual politics when it was taboo in cultures where machismo reigned supreme. His third novel *The Buenos Aires Affair* was censored and his life was threatened by right-wing militants. How can translating such writers not have political implications?

But already the act of challenging words is political because it makes us notice how they manipulate us, hence subversion, in my book, becomes a word for the translator to subvert. Sub-version: the word is dissected to reveal inside another meaning "version underneath," a potential version which the original imparts through the magical act of translation. Subversion in this context is also feminist insofar as it probes the hierarchy of original and translation and explores the semantic boundaries of language. Here I would like to note that there are some who have reproached me, as a woman translator, for translating male authors.

That (like most translators) I followed publishing trends and translated male writers is indisputable, but we can also argue that the men whose words I translated used language in ways that went against patriarchal models of language. Manuel Puig did not consider himself a feminist and yet made considerable contributions to his culture by questioning the rigid roles and definitions of gender and engaging his original readers in what was for them the unexplored terrain of homosexuality and sexual politics.

A translation will never be the text it imitates, which was written in another language, but it can be a version (virgin?) lying dormant and like Franken-stein's monster, animated by a mad translator (to use an Infantesque meta-phor), a text illuminated and motivated by the original, realized in its next life, in translation. Hence to speak of subversion is to stress creativity, that is, to set aside regretful talk of translation's shortcomings, secondariness or second sex—or any other label which would lead to that deadly cul de sac the linguist and literary theorist Roman Jakobson, with his thick Russian accent, grimly dismissed as "the dogma of untranslatability."

Translating Claudine Potvin's Pornographies or Searching for Eros

Anne Malena

This essay is based on my privileged experience of participating in the very first Banff International Literary Translation Centre residency in 2003 where I completed a draft of my translation of *Pornographies* amongst fellow practitioners all eager to share their own translating experience and provide advice when needed. This project and the Banff setting—its vista as much as its programme—brought me face to face with my inner self and demanded, particularly since I was translating from my mother tongue, French, into English, my adopted language, that this translation not betray the author, her text, or myself.

Many translators have been trained not to expose their own subjectivity and to remain invisible in order to allow the translation to fit smoothly into the target culture. Most texts, and many translators, resist this rule of thumb and Claudine Potvin's writing, because of its style and subject matter, proved particularly recalcitrant. *Pornographies* seeks to reveal the complexities of female subjectivity within a patriarchal system that encourages exploitation of the female body. The collection deals with the theme of pornography from a creative and poetic feminist perspective. As the epigraphs at the front of the book suggest, Potvin aims at weaving together Logos and Eros (Barthes) in a discourse suggestive of how meaningful pornography, "this spectacularly cramped form of the human imagination" (Sontag) can become when it is projected into art: "That discourse one might call the poetry of transgression is also knowledge" (Sontag). Potvin's writing, in enacting this search for knowledge in each of the eighteen stories, creates characters who transgress stereotypes and invites the readers to see hidden, and often beautiful, aspects within the pornographic images, all related to female power and agency that even the worst kinds of abuse cannot erase. Logos becomes fictive and is aesthetically nourished by the search for Eros. In this endeavour her writing follows in the footsteps of renowned Quebec avant–gardiste writers, such as Nicole Brossard or France Théoret, who have long made it their practice to blend theory and poetry, to weave together sensuality and intelligence and to build bridges between fiction and academia. Potvin's writing is self–reflexive and transgresses boundaries between writer and narrator, narrator and character, theory and fiction, male and female, dominatrix and victim, violence and

tenderness, pleasure and pain, conscious and unconscious, narration and description, monologue and dialogue. The result is an emphasis on how these oppositions are not mutually exclusive but always in dialogue with each other. Potvin pushes the limits of transgression further in (ab)using punctuation to lay open all the semantic possibilities of syntax; she plays voices with the virtuosity of a gypsy fiddler; she crosses back and forth between fiction and theory, using their colourful threads to weave the texture of her text. While translating I came to uncover hidden layers of meaning and reflect upon complex issues revealed by the dynamics between writing and translating.

Potvin's fiction revolves around issues of representation, cognition and aesthetics. The confrontation she creates between Pornê—from the ancient Greek πορνο, meaning a prostitute, something sold, akin to περνάναι, to sell (as a slave or for a bribe), to bring across, to come over—and Eros—the god of love, son of Aphrodite, a metonymic figure for sexual love or desire—is caught up in our human convoluted practices of representation, which in turn are embedded in our social, political and cultural practices. Potvin's book and my translation of it are, therefore, part and parcel of past, current and future debates about pornography, erotica, eroticism, writing, translation and representation. In choosing pornography as the theme for her book of short stories, Potvin seeks to transgress the stereotypes that this topic has come to represent and to reveal them as the gendered social and cultural constructs that they are. In translating, I sought to understand the multiple layers of representation and meaning she weaves together; I exposed the body of her French text and attempted to probe every one of its recesses before pulling over it the cover of the English language. The love I feel for the text does not shield it from the violence of my act of appropriation. What I can write about these stories, therefore, comes from this translation practice, which is also often described as one of the deepest forms of reading. As Elizabeth Grosz has pointed out, violence can be seen "as a positivity . . . in the domain of knowledges, reflection, thinking, and writing" (8). When Potvin rewrites the pornographic text, therefore, and I translate or rewrite her text, we are not offering a remedy to the violence of pornography but breaking the barriers that contain it; we transform it, letting it flow toward a future always open to transmutation. The search for Eros endlessly rewrites Pornê.

The accepted meaning of Pornê has evolved from the embodied subject of the prostitute or slave to the abstract notion of porn or "the production and selling of pictures and writings intended primarily to arouse sexual

desire" (Webster's). Eros has traveled along a parallel path to the notion of "erotic" or "arousing sexual feelings or desires; having to do with sexual love, amatory, highly susceptible to sexual stimulation" (Webster's). The OED gives slightly different definitions:

> *Pornography:* **The explicit description or exhibition of sexual subjects or activity in literature, painting, films, etc., in a manner intended to stimulate erotic rather than aesthetic feelings; printed or visual material containing this.**

> *Erotic:* **Of or pertaining to the passion of love; concerned with or treating of love; amatory.**

No clear opposition exists, therefore, between the two terms; they are intricately linked as the use of "erotic" in the above definition of pornography shows. Yet laws and other social discourses are formulated according to the supposed difference between the two terms, with "pornography" as a reprehensible practice and "erotic" raised to the enviable and untouchable level of art. In other words "pornography carries only one meaning—violence—and admits only one gaze—male" (Kostash 119). The Butler decision—the famous 1992 pronouncement by the Supreme Court of Canada, referred to in the epigraph of Potvin's story entitled "dominatrix"—has mostly failed to reduce the "degradation" and "harm" done to humans "from the free circulation of obscenity" (Kostash 120). Myrna Kostash opines that "the state is too blunt an instrument to make the distinction between nice 'erotica' and bad 'degradation'" (Kostash 121). In fact, six weeks after Butler rendered his decision, the Toronto Glad Day Bookstore, which carried *Bad Attitude,* a US "lesbian erotic fiction magazine," was charged and found guilty of selling obscene material (see Cossman et al. 4). The Butler decision did manage, however, to sharpen feminist debates and activism about the socio-economic consequences of heterosexual pornography on women. In *Bad Attitude/s on Trial: Pornography, Feminism, and the Butler Decision* (Cossman, Bell, Gotell and Ross), the collective seeks to demonstrate that anti-porn feminism is not a universally accepted feminist position. The authors stress that "[o]ur sexualities are complex and contradictory, always in the process of being constituted and reconstituted through a multiplicity of discourses, one of which is pornography" (25).

Potvin's short fictions illustrate this by focusing on the subjectivity of women involved in pornography, like the eponymous "dominatrix" who takes back the night, as it were, and struggles to gain control of her own body and mind in the heterosexual encounter. The outcome is not always

successful, and at times excruciatingly painful, but woman as subject is never in doubt. "dominatrix" starts with the following epigraph, taken from *Bad Attitude/s on Trial:* "Women in the sex industry—be it prostitution or the production of pornography—should be entitled to the same kind of employment protection that other workers are afforded" (53). In an unpublished introduction to this story, Potvin explains: "The dominatrix would not be this leather clad woman with chains traveling from the genitals to the breasts and wrists, pierced everywhere in her body, more or less vulgar, more or less grotesque, confused with the prostitute." Rather, she would be "sensitive, lucid, intelligent" and "work on her own pain," escaping the author who has to create Mirna, another authorial voice that quickly also loses control (1). Pornê is on the move, steps out of the frame; she is smarter than Mirna who, following her own desires and fantasies, keeps trying to bring her back into the more recognizable shape of a sadistic inflictor of pain. The dominatrix ends up writing herself "through sexual practices that almost always result in a feeling of uneasiness" ("Écrire" 2).

I, the translator, have to accompany the dominatrix into the English language and create a linguistic space for her without betraying her ambivalence. Such is my desire. Do I become obsessed with her? Do I end up completely identifying with her like Maude Laures in Brossard's *Désert mauve* identifies with Laure Angstelle, the fictional author of Désert mauve? Doing so would render translation impossible and make me confuse my dreams with reality, resolve the conflict of her subjectivity, take Brossard's fiction of translation as fact, sever the fragile thread maintaining the tension between the erotic and the pornographic and lose control of my act of appropriation. The violence the translator cannot help exerting on the text stems from the violence of language itself for what it cannot express and what it can only say badly. Language fails representation but reality, feelings and experiences persist in the writer/translator's desire to express them. Potvin does not write what she sees and I don't translate what I think she saw: we both struggle to let this multi-layered magma rise to the surface and let it be represented. As writer and translator we could describe ourselves as language workers—a bit like sex workers—that is, dealing with live and shifting matter. The danger is to remain within an impressionistic realm of representation, to turn pornographies into much too obvious samples of erotica. Most of all, translation does violence to the text because it risks tearing Pornê away from "graphy" and revealing the connecting threads within this intricate network of representation.

The most difficult story turned out to be "le *show* d'Angèle" because it draws the reader in and forces her to participate in the scopic exchange taking place between Angèle and her keepers. Mirna reappears here, struggling with the narration. Angèle is a child and there is a little sister, Colette, in the background; they play with their Barbie dolls during breaks in the filming of porn. Angèle has been in the movies since the age of 9. She is, of course, not (all) there. Mirna quotes Susanne Kappeler:

> The woman, object/victim par excellence in the structure of representation, is now being invited to join the readership and the spectators as a "voluntary audience" of the great cultural fiction—the patriarchy represented—now that the structure of representation, the scenario in representation, have been defined and confined to the transitive plot, the coercive imperative, now that the (male) gendered act of viewing and of reading has been naturalized
> (*The Pornography of Representation* 63).

Part of me, the translator, wants to deny Angèle her fictive voice, manipulate the representation of this subject wrapped in pain to return to a zone of comfort where I don't have to look at this scene any more. My impulse is to turn away from this raw exposure of the pornographic scene. Mirna is no longer in control: "she interrupts the story. Bent over the text. Angèle's body bursts onto the page." She walks away, turns on the television and the screen throws at her the image of a fake reality, arranged in advance. She goes back to her text: "Mirna questions the porphyroid texture of her obscene angel story. The cliché of the fallen angel she thinks" (*Pornographies* 65).

I, in turn, cannot finish the translation. I go for a walk. I interrogate my violent reaction to the text and my conflicting emotions about the representation of this pornographic subject. Why, why did she have to use a child? The filming stops, the text comes to an end: Mirna receives Angèle's show like a whipping. The red lines on her cheek inscribing a kind of cinematographic writing at the exact point of exploit(ation) (*Pornographies* 68).

Potvin herself told me in Banff about the uneasiness she felt about this text when she read my draft. Is it possible to go too far in wanting to expose the pornographic scene and inscribe female subjectivity within it? Is the search for Eros necessarily bound to fail? Is the representation of representation inevitably pornographic? Deep down we know how fragile Angèle's agency is and that no matter how hard we push language, how well we master the graphy, Pornê remains beyond our reach.

Word choice, sentence structure, narrative voices and more also form part of the translator's struggle with her own desires and subjectivity as each detail potentially affects the creativity of the source text and threatens to shift it. The most striking examples I encountered in *Pornographies* had to do with what I inwardly referred to as "angels and sex" and "fun puns." The figures of genderless angels and cherubs provide Potvin with a wonderful transgressing device to blur the boundaries between Logos and Eros, sacred and profane, love and sex, female and male. Since French is a heavily gendered language it is relatively simple to turn the little neutral, celestial figures into subversive females. For example, in "qui est–elle l'ange du plateau l'Ang/elle qui joue la scène sadomasochiste de ses fantasmes enfantins l'aile du désir le regard d'une enfante sourde et muette" the mark of the feminine, "elle," is easily rendered by the literal "she," followed by "her" for "ses" and the repetitious play on Ang/elle by the proper name Angela ("aquatinte", *Pornographies* 11; my emphasis). I remember breathing a sigh of relief and gratitude for the propensity of English names to Latinate endings. In the case of "enfante," however, the stakes were higher. French has very few neutral words but "enfant" is one and the neologism "enfante," therefore, typical of Potvin's creativity, marks the feminine and lends the figure a slight tone of royalty by sounding very close to "infante," a word derived from Spanish designating the youngest child in a royal family. To translate the feminine is simple through the use of "her" but "child" for "enfante" registers a loss.

Paradoxically, a certain pleasure can be derived from admitting defeat. A problem in "Angèle's Show" made me smile every time I struggled with it, a welcome relief, given the difficulty of this particular story. Potvin's wit and the resistance of language to submit are admirable: *"Angèle se débauche un peu trop au goût de son père. Danse sur une corde raide qui ne lui appartient plus, s'initie* **au jeu du chat et lui sourit** (*Pornographies* 67; my emphasis). A literal, albeit polysemic, translation would be: "the game of the cat and smiles at him/her". In French the game allows for a play between the maleness of the cat and the homonym of mouse/smiles, which highlights the opposition between father, and his implied complicity with male predatory desire, and daughter. The homonymic possibility that *"lui sourit"* means "him the mouse", could imply that Angela becomes the cat and her father the mouse, thus increasing her agency. My solution, "the game of cat and mouse", is far from perfect but retains the idea of power.

In conclusion, loss and transformation are inevitable in translation. The challenge is to minimize losses and make creative use of transformation. The excitement of confronting the creator's challenges never abates and anxiety is richly compensated by the pleasure of searching for solutions. Perhaps this is where Logos can briefly find Eros.

La « double conscience » du traducteur

Patricia Godbout

J'aimerais livrer ici quelques réflexions qui émanent d'un projet de traduction que je viens de terminer. Il s'agit de la version française de l'essai de Winfried Siemerling *The New North American Studies* (paru chez Routledge en 2005), qui vient de paraître aux Presses de l'Université Laval, sous le titre *Récits nord-américains d'émergence*. Publié au moment où la tendance générale à la mondialisation de nombreuses sphères d'activité suscite une réflexion sur la notion de frontière, l'essai de Siemerling aborde de nombreux débats littéraires contemporains (comme ceux sur les canons littéraires, les questions d'identité et de multiculturalisme) dans une perspective nord-américaine et non plus seulement nationale (canadienne ou états-unienne, par exemple). Or, le fait de transporter — par le biais de la traduction — ce débat dans une autre sphère linguistique fait ressortir une territorialité propre à l'espace francophone quant à la mise en circulation de maints concepts et idées dont traite Siemerling dans son livre.

Importation littéraire

Il me paraît intéressant à cet égard de parler — plutôt que de simple traduction — d'une activité plus vaste d'importation littéraire. L'historien français Blaise Wilfert définit celle-ci comme l'ensemble des pratiques liées à l'introduction d'une œuvre, d'une réputation, d'un texte littéraires étrangers dans un nouveau champ intellectuel donné. Il rappelle que les transferts intellectuels peuvent précéder, et de loin, les traductions des œuvres étrangères dans l'espace culturel qui les reçoit, par le biais de correspondances, de sociabilités, de la circulation des livres dans leur langue originale. En fait, ce serait bien souvent la référence étrangère qui produirait en quelque sorte, peu à peu, la nécessité de la traduction : pour peu que le texte étranger participe décisivement au débat intellectuel local, il devient inévitable de le traduire. La nécessité de la transcription dans la langue de l'importateur et de ses lecteurs s'impose de ce fait assez rapidement. C'est précisément dans cette opération que le traducteur fait le geste socialement et intellectuellement significatif, pour lui et pour l'ensemble des acteurs du champ littéraire, qui est de faire advenir, d'une manière ou d'une autre, un nouveau texte en langue nationale, susceptible donc d'intégrer le capital de textes et de références qui fonde la mémoire et le capital du champ, mais à partir de la position excentrée d'une signature d'étranger.

The Double Consciousness of Translators

Patricia Godbout

I would like to share some reflections arising from a translation project I have just completed. I translated into French Winfried Siemerling's essay *The New North American Studies* (Routledge, 2005) which was recently published by Presses de l'Université Laval under the title *Récits nord-américains d'émergence* (2010, 318 p.). Published when the general trend toward the globalization of numerous spheres of activity leads to questions around the notion of borders, Siemerling's essay tackles several contemporary literary debates (concerning literary canons, issues of identity and multiculturalism, for instance) from a North American and not solely national (Canadian or US, for instance) perspective. By bringing the debate into another linguistic sphere through translation, I became aware of the territoriality present in the Francophone space concerning the diffusion of many of the concepts and ideas dealt with in Siemerling's book.

Literary Imports

Rather than addressing my remarks to translation alone, I would like to speak of an activity much greater than translation itself—that of literary imports. French historian Blaise Wilfert defines this as the combination of practices linked to the introduction of a foreign work, reputation, or literary text into a new intellectual field. He points out that intellectual transfers occur over what is often a long period prior to the translation of foreign works through the exchange of correspondence, social inter-action and the circulation of books in their original language. In actual fact, references made to a foreign work often gradually feed into the need to translate it; insofar as a foreign text participates decisively in the local intellectual debate, translating it becomes inevitable. The resulting need to transcribe the text in the importing language for its readers soon becomes apparent. During the operation itself, translators carry out the social and intellectual act of importance both for the translator and all literary partici-pants, that of bringing a new text from the excentric position of an out-sider to a field into the national language's field to become part of the capital of texts and references composing that field.

La traduction s'inscrit ainsi dans un continuum de pratiques qui l'entourent et lui donnent une part essentielle de son sens historique. Au côté du travail du traducteur, il faut donc être aussi attentif à celui de chroniqueurs, de directeurs de collections de littérature étrangère, de compilateurs de portraits d'auteurs ou de courants littéraires, etc. Il pourrait être intéressant, à titre d'exemple, de voir quels sont les « agents » au sein de presses universitaires comme celle de l'University of Minnesota Press qui sont derrière « l'importation » de plusieurs titres français et allemands d'auteurs comme Hélène Cixous, Catherine Clément, Gilles Deleuze, Michel de Certeau, mais aussi Jauss, Brecht et Adorno.

La traduction du livre de Siemerling m'a permis de voir, pour ma part, à partir des titres les plus souvent cités par l'auteur, lesquels avaient été traduits en français et lesquels ne l'avaient pas été. La liste de ces derniers s'est avérée plus longue que je ne l'aurais cru. En effet, ce petit relevé m'a permis de constater que la liste d'essayistes non traduits en français inclut des noms aussi prestigieux que ceux de Houston A. Baker, Henry Louis Gates, Hortense Spillers et Sacvan Bercovitch, mais aussi, plus près de nous au Canada, E. D. Blodgett, George Elliott Clarke et Linda Hutcheon. J'ai par contre pu constater qu'au cours des quinze dernières années, les ouvrages de plusieurs auteurs ayant traité de questions d'identité nationale et de postmodernisme avait été traduits : notons en particulier *L'imaginaire national* de Benedict Anderson (1996), *Ces merveilleuses possessions* de Stephen Jay Greenblatt (1996), *L'orientalisme* d'Edward Saïd (un an plus tard, au Seuil, avec une préface de Tzvetan Todorov), et, beaucoup plus récemment, *Le postmodernisme ou la logique culturelle du capitalisme tardif* de Fredric Jameson (2007).

Dans un chapitre des *Récits nord-américains d'émergence* intitulé « L'écriture autochtone, l'oralité et la traduction anti-impérialiste : Thomas King et Gerald Vizenor », Siemerling traite plus particulièrement des littératures autochtones d'Amérique du Nord. Le rôle d'une collection comme « Terre indienne » dirigée par Francis Geffard chez Albin Michel apparaît nettement comme étant un haut lieu d'importation littéraire. Par exemple, plusieurs titres de Thomas King (*Medicine River, Monroe Swimmer est de retour, L'herbe verte, l'eau vive*) y ont été publiés dans la traduction française d'Hugues Leroy. (Mentionnons que ce traducteur a fait un séjour en 2005 à la résidence annuelle du Centre international de traduction littéraire de Banff : ce fut notamment pour lui une occasion de voir ce fameux Ouest canadien où se situe une partie de l'action des romans de King.)

Thus, translation is part of a continuum of related practices that give it an essential part of its historical meaning. Along with the focus on the translator's work, attention must also be paid to the work of chroniclers, directors of foreign literature series, compilers of author portraits or literary movements, etc. It would be interesting, for instance, to see which "agents" within university presses such as the University of Minnesota Press are responsible for "importing" several French and German authors such as Hélène Cixous, Catherine Clément, Gilles Deleuze and Michel de Certeau as well as Jauss, Brecht and Adorno.

As I translated Siemerling's book, I was able to see, among the titles most often cited by the author, which had been translated into French and which had not. There were more of the latter than I would have thought. My count showed that the list of essay writers not translated into French includes names as prestigious as Houston A. Baker, Henry Louis Gates, Hortense Spillers and Sacvan Bercovitch and, closer to home in Canada, E.D. Blodgett, George Elliott Clarke and Linda Hutcheon. I did see, however, that over the past fifteen years, the works of several authors on issues of national identity and postmodernism have been translated, particularly, Benedict Anderson's *Imagined Communities: Reflections on the Origin and Spread of Nationalism* (1991) (*L'imaginaire national* published in 1996), Stephen Jay Greenblatt's *Marvelous Possessions: The Wonder of the New World* (1992) (*Ces merveilleuses possessions*, published in 1996), Edward Saïd's *Orientalism*, 1978 (*L'orientalisme* published by Seuil in 1997 with a preface from Tzvetan Todorov) and, much more recently, Fredric Jameson's *Postmodernism, or, The Cultural Logic of Late Capitalism* (1991) (*Le postmodernisme ou la logique culturelle du capitalisme tardif*, published in 2007).

In a chapter of *The New North American Studies* entitled "Aboriginal Writing, Orality and Anti-Imperialist Translation: Thomas King and Gerald Vizenor," Siemerling deals more specifically with the aboriginal literatures of North America. The role of a collection such as "Terre indienne" edited by Francis Geffard at Albin Michel, is of prime importance for literary imports. For instance, several titles by Thomas King (*Medicine River, Truth and Bright Water* and *Green Grass, Running Water*) were published in a French translation by Hugues Leroy. A note in passing: the latter attended the 2005 BILTC residency and was able to see for himself the famous Canadian West, the setting for a good portion of King's novels.

La traduction de romans d'auteurs amérindiens comme Leslie Marmon Silko, N. Scott Momaday, James Welch ou Gerald Vizenor s'inscrit dans un courant d'intérêt, en France, pour cette littérature autochtone nord-américaine de langue anglaise. Un recueil de nouvelles amérindiennes réunies par Vizenor a d'ailleurs été publié tout récemment chez Métailié. On se désole cependant du choix du titre même — *Des nouvelles des Indiens d'Amérique du Nord* —, lequel est problématique à cause de toutes les réflexions de Vizenor sur « l'invention de l'Indien » par les Blancs. De plus, il me semble qu'on ne peut pas, comme le fait le traducteur, parler en français de conteurs « natifs » ni de narrations « natives », même si l'adjectif est mis entre guillemets.

Dans le champ de la littérature africaine américaine, la publication toute récente de traductions françaises de titres importants, anciens et plus près de nous dans le temps, est significative : notons, parmi les auteurs traduits, Booker T. Washington en 2008, pendant la plus récente campagne présidentielle américaine; Frederick Douglass et Zora Neale Hurston en 2006; Paul Gilroy, *L'Atlantique noir*, en 2003, de même que Ralph Ellison : *Homme invisible, pour qui chantes-tu?*, la même année. Le fait que certains titres ne sont parus en traduction française que bien des années après la publication en langue originale est le plus souvent présenté dans les recensions en termes de décalage ou de retard. Cela ne prend toutefois pas en compte qu'un espace littéraire donné obéit dans une assez large mesure à une logique qui lui est propre, logique à laquelle même les activités d'importation littéraire sont subordonnées. Pour qu'une œuvre étrangère soit importée et traduite, il faut qu'un certain nombre de conditions soient réunies. C'est à mon avis la dynamique propre au champ importateur qui est primordiale. Dans une telle perspective, parler de retard ou de décalage n'a pas beaucoup de sens.

W. E. B. Du Bois en traduction française

La parution la plus significative dans le champ des études africaines-américaines est sans contredit la traduction, en 2004, par Magali Bessone, des *Âmes du peuple noir* de W. E. B. Du Bois (Le Découverte, traduction rééditée au format de poche en 2007). Publié au départ en 1903, ce recueil d'essais de Du Bois est un ouvrage capital « qui fonde la conscience politique noire américaine », écrit la traductrice dans une introduction intitulée « Pourquoi lire Du Bois aujourd'hui en France ? ».

Une notion hégélienne centrale chez Du Bois, de même que dans le chapitre des *Récits nord-américains d'émergence* qui en traite, est celle de

Translations of the work of North American aboriginal writers like Leslie Marmon Silko, N. Scott Momaday, James Welch or Gerald Vizenor are part of a surge of interest in France for English-language aboriginal literature. In fact, a collection of aboriginal short stories chosen by Vizenor was published quite recently by Métailié. The title is unfortunate and problematic, however—*Des nouvelles des Indiens d'Amérique du Nord*—because of Vizenor's many comments on white culture's "invention of the Indian." The translator's use in French, with or without quotation marks, of the adjective "natif/native" (which is not a synonym for aboriginal as it is in English) when speaking of writers or stories seems to pose another problem.

As for African-American literature, the recent publication in French of important titles, old and new, is significant: among translated authors we find Booker T. Washington during the most recent US presidential campaign in 2008; Frederick Douglass and Zora Neale Hurston in 2006; Paul Gilroy, *The Black Atlantic: Modernity and Double Consciousness* (1992) (*L'Atlantique noir*, published in 2003) and Ralph Ellison, *Invisible Man* (1952) (*Homme invisible, pour qui chantes-tu?* published in 2003 as well). The fact that some of these titles appeared in translation many years after the original publication is usually explained in reviews in terms of a time lag or delay. This, however, does not take into account the fact that any given literary space in large part obeys its own logic, to which even literary importing activities are subordinated. For a foreign literary work to be imported and translated, a certain number of conditions have to come together. In my opinion, it is the dynamic within the importing country that is more important. From that perspective, time lags or delays do not make much sense.

W.E.B. Du Bois in French translation

The most important French translation in the field of African-American studies is without doubt Magali Bessone's *Les Âmes du peuple noir* (La Découverte, 2004, a translation re-issued in pocket book format in 2007) of the book by W.E.B. Du Bois *The Souls of Black Folk*. Originally published in 1903, Du Bois's collection of essays is a work of capital importance, serving as "the basis for black American political consciousness" as stated by the translator in the introduction entitled "Why Read Du Bois in France today?"

A central Hegelian notion in both Du Bois and the relevant chapter in *The New North American Studies*, is that of *Aufhebung*, which,

l'*Aufhebung*, qui est, dans ses grandes lignes, ce mouvement par lequel la thèse et l'antithèse tendent vers la synthèse. Le mot *Aufhebung* comporterait en allemand les deux sens en apparence contradictoires de préserver et de modifier (le verbe allemand *aufheben* signifie à la fois soulever, lever, garder ; et abolir, annuler, par exemple une loi). La tension entre ces deux sens servirait le propos de Hegel. Dans le contexte de la dialectique, il aurait ainsi voulu dire les deux. Par l'entremise de l'*Aufhebung*, un terme ou concept est à la fois préservé et modifié au moyen d'une interaction dialectique avec un autre terme ou concept. Si l'on veut, l'*Aufhebung* est le moteur qui permet à la dialectique de fonctionner.

Siemerling s'intéresse à la façon dont Du Bois est parvenu, dans *Les Âmes du peuple noir*, à opérer une « évasion de l'équation » (2005, p. 8) — ou un maintien de la différence. Du Bois souhaitait réaliser l'intégration dialectique de tous les éléments de sa propre expérience mais il se rendit compte que ce n'était pas possible, ce qui le conduisit à son concept de « double conscience ». Citons Du Bois dans la traduction de Magali Bessone :

> **L'histoire du Noir américain est l'histoire de [...] cette aspiration à être un homme conscient de lui-même, de cette volonté de fondre son moi double en un seul moi meilleur et plus vrai. Dans cette fusion, il ne veut perdre aucun de ses anciens moi. Il ne voudrait pas africaniser l'Amérique, car l'Amérique a trop à enseigner au monde et à l'Afrique. Il ne voudrait pas décolorer son âme noire dans un flot d'américanisme blanc, car il sait qu'il y a dans le sang noir un message pour le monde (Du Bois, 2007, p. 11-12).**

Siemerling repère dans la pensée duboisienne une ambiguïté non résolue entre abolition dialectique et différence dialogique, cette dernière permettant de conserver les contradictions dans une tension dynamique.

Si l'on compare, dans la perspective proposée par le livre de Siemerling, les principaux choix qui s'offrent au traducteur pour traduire le mot *Aufhebung*, on voit qu'on a le choix ou bien de conserver l'*Aufhebung* allemand, ou bien d'aller vers l'une ou l'autre des traductions proposées par les traducteurs français de la *Phénoménologie de l'Esprit* : la dyade « suppression / dépassement » pour Jean Hyppolite (1946), version lue par Jean-Paul Sartre et toute une génération d'intellectuels français, et le terme « abolition » proposé par Jean-Pierre Lefebvre dans sa traduction parue en 1991.

Le choix fait par Jean Hippolyte de recourir aux deux mots suppression / dépassement pour traduire *Aufhebung* s'accorde avec une vision de l'histoire perçue comme une succession de cycles, ou de moments

generally speaking, is where thesis and antithesis move toward synthesis. The German word *Aufhebung* ["sublation" in English] holds two seemingly contradictory meanings of preserving and modifying (the German verb *aufheben* means both to lift up, raise, keep and to abolish or rescind, a law for instance). The tension between the two meanings fits Hegel's discourse. In the dialectical context, he meant both. Through *Aufhebung*, a term or concept is both preserved and modified by dialectical interaction with another term or concept. In other words, *Aufhebung* is the engine that allows dialectics to function.

Siemerling is interested in how Du Bois managed to stage an "evasion of the equation" (2005, 8) in *The Souls of Black Folk*; that is, how he managed to retain difference. Du Bois hoped to effect a dialectical integration of all elements from his own experience but realized the impossibility of the venture, leading him to the concept of "double consciousness." Below is a quote from Du Bois:

> The history of the American Negro is the history of [...] this longing to attain self-conscious manhood, to merge his double self into a better, truer self. In this merging he wishes neither of the older selves to be lost. He would not Africanize America, because America has too much to teach the world and Africa. They do not bleach his Negro soul in a flood of white Americanism, for he knows that Negro blood has a message for the world (Du Bois, quoted in Siemerling 2005, 34-35).

Siemerling points out the unresolved ambiguity in Du Bois's approach between dialectic abolition and dialogic difference, the latter making it possible to maintain contradictions in a dynamic tension.

To follow Siemerling's perspective and compare the major choices offered a translator to translate the word *Aufhebung* into French, the choice is clearly between keeping the German word or adopting either of two translations proposed by the French translators of Hegel's *The Phenomenology of Spirit*: the "*suppression/dépassement*" dyad by Jean Hyppolite (Aubier-Montaigne, 1946)—the version read by Jean-Paul Sartre and an entire generation of French intellectuals—and the term "*abolition*" proposed by Jean-Pierre Lefebvre in his 1991 translation (Aubier).

Jean Hippolyte's decision to use the two words *suppression/dépassement* to translate *Aufhebung* fits with a vision of history as a series of cycles or dialectical moments that give rise to an irreversible linear movement

dialectiques, qui engendreront un irréversible mouvement linéaire assurant la pleine réalisation de l'Esprit et, par le fait même, la pleine réalisation de l'humanité. Pour Jean-Pierre Lefebvre, toutefois, cette dyade ne pouvait convenir. Dans son glossaire, le traducteur écrit qu'il a traduit systématiquement le verbe *aufheben* par « abolir » et *Aufhebung* par « abolition ». Il explique que ce dernier mot est pour lui une « mise hors de vigueur, de présence, ou d'actualité, sans qu'il y ait nécessairement destruction et/ou réduction à néant » (Hegel, 1991, p. 529). Ce mot pointerait déjà dans la direction des ambiguïtés et des non-résolutions entre abolition dialectique et différence dialogique qu'on observe dans la pensée duboisienne telle qu'examinée par Siemerling. De plus, les résonances particulières (liées au mouvement abolitionniste) de l'équivalent français proposé par Jean-Pierre Lefebvre dans le contexte précis dont discute Siemerling iraient dans le sens souhaité, si l'on veut.

On connaît aussi la contribution à ce chapitre de Jacques Derrida, qui a proposé le mot « relève » pour traduire Aufhebung (et « relever » pour *aufheben*). Dans *Qu'est-ce qu'une traduction « relevante »?*, Derrida explique que c'est à l'occasion d'une conférence qu'il avait prononcée en janvier 1968 au Collège de France dans le séminaire de Jean Hyppolite que ce mot s'était imposé à lui « pour traduire (sans traduire) » la notion hégélienne d'*Aufhebung* (Derrida, 2005, p. 76-77). Derrida rappelle que ce mot « capital et à double sens de Hegel » signifie à la fois supprimer et élever; c'est « un mot dont Hegel dit qu'il représente une chance spéculative de la langue allemande, un mot que tout le monde s'accordait jusque-là pour trouver intraduisible » (p. 64). Pour Derrida, ce mouvement d'*Aufhebung*, ce processus « relevant » est toujours chez Hegel un mouvement dialectique de mémoire intériorisante et de spiritualisation sublimante (p. 65).

Affirmant son admiration « pour ceux et celles que je tiens pour les seuls à savoir lire et écrire : les traductrices et les traducteurs » (p. 8), Derrida s'interroge sur ce qu'on devrait tenir pour une traduction « relevante ». L'emploi adjectival de « relevant » en français donne aussitôt à penser qu'il s'agit d'une francisation implicite de l'adjectif anglais « relevant ». Comme le note Derrida, ce mot qui se voit confier la tâche de définir l'essence de la traduction « porte en son corps, une opération de traduction en cours » (p. 14). Selon lui, toute traduction donnée, la meilleure et la pire, se tient entre la « relevance » (transparence) absolue et « l'irrelevance » la plus opaque (p. 20-21). Une traduction « relevante » élève et remplace, conserve ce qu'elle détruit, garde ce qu'elle fait disparaître.

toward full realization of the Spirit, and thus of humanity. For Jean-Pierre Lefebvre, however, the dyad was not enough. In his glossary, the translator writes that he systematically translated the verb *aufheben* with "*abolir*" and *Aufhebung* with "*abolition*." He explains that, in his view, the latter is a "displacement in force, presence or importance without necessarily amounting to the destruction and/or reduction to nothing" (Hegel, 1991, 529). The word itself points to the ambiguity and non-resolution between dialectical abolition and dialogic distinction as seen in Du Bois's approach and examined by Siemerling. Furthermore, the specific resonances (linked to the abolitionist movement) of the French equivalent proposed by Jean-Pierre Lefebvre points in the right direction, so to speak, in the specific context discussed by Siemerling.

Jacques Derrida has also contributed to the debate, proposing the word "*relève*" to translate Aufhebung and "*relever*" for *aufheben*. In "*Qu'est-ce qu'une traduction "relevante"?* (Cahiers de l'Herne, 2005), Derrida explains that it was during a talk he gave in January 1968 at the Collège de France in Jean Hyppolite's class that the word first came to him as a way "to translate (without translating) the Hegelian notion of *Aufhebung*" (Derrida, 2005, 76-77). Derrida points out that "Hegel's all-important two-pronged term" means both *supprimer* and *élever*; it is "a word that, according to Hegel, represents a speculative opportunity provided by the German language that everyone until then had agreed was untranslatable" (64). For Derrida, the movement of *Aufhebung*, the "*relevant*" process, is always, in Hegel, a dialectical movement of interiorizing memory and sublimating spiritualization (65).

Stating his admiration "for the only beings knowledgable in reading and writing, i.e. translators" (8), Derrida wonders what should be seen as a "*relevant*" translation. At first glance, the use of "*relevant*" as an adjective in French might seem like a gallicization of the English adjective "relevant." As Derrida points out, the word designed to define the essence of translation "carries inside its body an ongoing translation operation" (14). In his view, any translation, the best and the worst, is found somewhere between absolute "relevance" (transparence) and the most opaque "irrelevance" (20-21). A "*relevant*" translation erects and replaces, maintains what it destroys, and retains what it causes to disappear.

Un double mouvement d'intériorisation et de spiritualisation

Tentant de prendre la mesure de la part d'indécidable inhérente à la notion derridienne de « relevance » en traduction, je me demande à mon tour si l'on ne pourrait pas appliquer à la situation du traducteur la notion duboisienne de « double conscience », telle qu'elle est exposée par Siemerling. Dans la perspective dialectique hégélienne, la production d'un texte cible constitue une sorte de « produit de synthèse » dans lequel la phase antithétique de la traduction disparaît pour permettre la diffusion d'un auteur « étranger » dans un autre espace littéraire et, par là, dans l'espace littéraire mondial. La « double conscience » du traducteur inciterait plutôt ce dernier à tenir en état de tension et de dialogue, à maintenir, de fait, en vie des éléments qui, autrement, ont tendance à s'exclure mutuellement : la pleine prise en compte de l'esprit et de la lettre du texte source, d'une part, et leur transférabilité dans le texte et la langue cibles, d'autre part.

Cette « double conscience » ne participe pas d'emblée à la fabrication d'une « littérature mondiale » désincarnée et dépouillée de tout attribut circonstancié. Elle reconnaît le caractère sensible de la tâche du traducteur, qui est à la fois intériorisation (lecture et interprétation du texte source) et spiritualisation (création d'un nouveau texte qui conserve néanmoins *l'esprit de la lettre* de « l'ancien »). Le traducteur animé de cette double conscience voudrait produire une traduction qui ne soit ni tout à fait « relevante » (c'est-à-dire qui pratique la domestication, au sens où l'entend Lawrence Venuti — traducteur de Derrida — ou qui « décolore l'âme » du texte source, pour paraphraser Du Bois, ni tout à fait « irrelevante » (qui pratique la défamiliarisation à tout prix).   Partout où l'unité du mot est menacée ou mise en question, écrit Derrida, c'est l'idée de la traduction qu'il faut reconsidérer (2005, p. 27). La « double conscience » du traducteur suppose la reconsidération des idées préconçues sur soi et sur l'autre. Elle invite à interroger la certitude de soi et à participer à la re-définition des identités. Les effets de traduction produits par cette double conscience sont particulièrement intéressants à observer, me semble-t-il, tels qu'ils se manifestent dans l'espace nord-américain qu'explorent tant le livre de Siemerling, *Récits nord-américains d'émergence,* que le Centre international de traduction littéraire de Banff.

The double movement of internalization and spiritualization

As I reflect on the concept of "undecidability" inherent in the Derridian notion of "relevance" in translation, I also wonder whether the Duboisian notion of "double consciousness" as presented by Siemerling could not be applied to the translator's situation. In the Hegelian dialectical view, the production of a target text is the product of a synthesis in which the translation's antithetical phase disappears to allow for the diffusion of a "foreign" author within another literary space and, consequently, in the global literary space. However, the translator's "double consciousness" would incite her to keep elements in a state of tension and dialogue, thus keeping alive elements which otherwise tend to be mutually exclusive: fully taking into account the spirit and the letter of the source text, on the one hand, and their transferability into the target text and language, on the other.

The "double consciousness" does not create a disembodied "global literature" stripped of any circumstantial attributes. It acknowledges the delicate nature of the translator's task, that of both internalizing (reading and interpreting the source text) and spiritualizing (creating a new text that nevertheless maintains the spirit of the letter of the initial text) the text. Guided by double consciousness, the translator strives to produce a translation that is neither wholly "relevant" (in other words, domesticated in the sense used by translation studies scholar Lawrence Venuti—who is also one of Derrida's translators—or "soul-bleaching" of the source text to paraphrase Du Bois), or wholly "irrelevant" (defamiliarizing at all costs). Derrida writes that whenever a word's unity is questioned or threatened, translation itself needs to be reconsidered (2005, 27). The translator's "double consciousness" requires a re-examination of preconceived ideas around oneself and the other. It means questioning one's certainty and redefining identities. The translation effects of double consciousness are of particular interest, it seems to me, as manifested in the North American space explored both by Siemerling's book *The New North American Studies* and at the Banff International Literary Translation Centre.

Translation by S. Ouriou

Literary Translation into the Indigenous Languages of the Americas

Enrique Servín Herrera

I will start with a short poem composed some six hundred years ago by Nezahualcoyotl, one of the last rulers of the kingdom of Texcoco, in Ancient Mexico:

Tel ca chalchihuitl no xamani,
 no teocuitlatl in tlapani,
no quetzalli poztequi.
Ya hui ohuaya:
An nochipa tlalticpac
zan achica ye nican.

Even precious stones shatter
Even gold can break
Even quetzal feathers crumble
Alas, Alas:
We are not forever on the Earth
but only for the briefest moment

Literature flourished in the region during that period as far as we can judge from the very few examples that survived the Spanish Conquest, such as this poem. The language in which it was composed, Classical Náhuatl, also called Mexican, or more rarely Aztec, is just one of many belonging to the so-called Uto-Aztec linguistic family, which, in turn, is just one of dozens of linguistic families native to a huge continent that stretches almost from pole to pole. This diversity encompasses, of course, many different traits and sociolinguistic situations, but all of the indigenous languages of the Americas, as diverse as they may be, share several general characteristics of a very distinct nature: first is the fact that from the structural point of view they are strikingly different from Indo-European (or even from Old World Languages in general); second is the minority status they are relegated to in almost all the countries where they are spoken; and last but not least, the undeniable condition of being either "rural-constrained," or, even since the sixteenth century, "hegemonized languages," that is, communication codes that were expelled from and deprived of complex urban environments—wherever this was once the case—or steadily kept apart from them. This means, among other things, that for the last five hundred years they have been almost completely absent from the

world of higher education, modern science and technology, as well as the spheres of higher political power. All of this accounts for the special difficulties a translator faces when working with, for example, Cree, spoken from eastern to western Canada, or Yaqui, spoken in the Mexican state of Sonora.

Indigenous languages may contain a bewildering abundance of terms regarding their geographical habitat or the social structures of the communities in which they are spoken, but they usually lack equivalents for most of the terms used in other languages when describing almost anything pertaining to a modern environment. An English sentence as simple as "When I heard a ring, I went to the desk and answered the phone" can be frustratingly difficult to translate into Tarahumara, since this language has always been used in an environment where there is no ring, no desk and no phone. Furthermore, the fact that there were, until recently, no linguistic authorities within indigenous communities, such as a school system based on the use of aboriginal languages, or an official academy regulating aspects such as orthography or grammatical and lexical variation, has kept alive the natural dialectal diversity, so important from many points of view, but nevertheless an obstacle to the development of written literature.

Literary writing and literary translation into the aboriginal languages of the Americas are certainly not new phenomena. They thrived even up to the sixteenth century, when cathechisms, biblical texts, laws and even theological and scientific treatises were written in Classical and Colonial Náhuatl. Virgil's *Eclogue IV*, for instance, is available in Náhuatl. The consolidation of Spanish rule by the end of the seventeenth century nearly put an end to that activity. But the renaissance of aboriginal languages as literary media of expression—setting aside the fascinating subject of traditional oral literatures—is indeed a novelty in the recent panorama of Latin-American culture. Indigenous creative writing began during the 1980s (in some cases somewhat earlier), and in the short span of only three decades has already produced several interesting writers and oeuvres. We cannot be sure, of course, what the outcome of this literary movement will be in the long term, but if we want this fascinating process to consolidate and serve as a strategy for preserving our cultural diversity, literary translation into the indigenous languages will certainly have to play an important role.

Yet, given the above mentioned difficulties, some questions arise. Is a modern French novel translatable into the Yaqui language? Definitely. But not without making abundant use of strategies and resources that are

generally avoided by the standard translator, such as footnoting, word-loaning, loan-translation, circumloquia, adaptation and plain omission, while risking having the traditional autochthonous readership understand little, or, in the best of cases, only part of the translation. Another question: Is the role of the translator when translating from and to "modern" (or *non*-hegemonized languages) the same as when translating from French into Yaqui? Definitely not, because in the former case the translator works with culturally interconnected codes and within a well-established tradition, whereas in the latter he or she often faces a real cultural chasm and operates as an intermediary and as one of the *inventors* of a written literary tradition. The pressure caused by these circumstances often invites and even forces him or her to perform acts of social intervention, thus transcending the mere function of what we call translation. In other words, any such enterprise may well be an exercise of cultural adaptation and language alteration.

All literary languages differ from spoken forms, which are nothing but an everchanging continuum of interconnected codes that vary not only according to region, but also to social class, age group and even individuals. When writers develop or accept a "standard variety," what they are doing is trying to freeze a language form, both in space (geographically) and in time (diachronically), so that it can become a common ground for a whole community for at least one period of history. We all know that this frozen language block is not really a "block" and is not really "frozen"; we know that it needs impurities and is always cracking and melting away, until eventually it is abandoned and replaced by a newer form. The history of Latin is a good example of this. But in the mid-term, a literary standard has become a successful means to develop and maintain a whole literature. The problem with most minority and hegemonized languages is that they have no such literary form, and whatever a translator or indigenous writer produces is contributing, whether intentionally or not, to the *creation* of that standard. In other words, both the indigenous writer and even more so the literary translator into indigenous languages act as *language planners*, sometimes starting out by establishing an orthography, but more often than not choosing between different dialect forms, giving new meaning to old words and expressions, accepting or rejecting loans or calques, and even creating new words.

Two of the most troublesome questions in this process are plain adaptation and vocabulary expansion. Natural languages are, as we all know, assymetrical amongst themselves, and the further they are separated from the philogenetic and cultural points of view, the more assymetrical they can be.

When we compare the vocabulary of a language such as Tarahumara with that of a well-established literary language, the lack of clear-cut correspondences can eventually lead to the one-way solution of adaptation. Japanese distinguishes between "whirlpools" and "whirlwinds," just as English and Spanish do. But Tarahumara, spoken in a geographic area where "whirlpools" are unheard of, has only one term, equivalent to "whirlwind." Upon translating Ono no Komachi's famous tanka poem in which the poetess compares herself to a floating lotus and complains about her solitude, wishing to follow a whirlpool, the Tarahumara poetess Dolores Batista faced a problem: in the Tarahumara sierras there are no lotuses and no whirlpools, and therefore no words for them. Adding notes or new coined words would only add artificiality into a very short poem and thus neutralize it as a poem, so that was not an option. The only way out was an adaptation. The final result, retranslated into English, reads more or less as follows: "Always alone/ wind carries me away like a fallen flower. / Sad and alone./ Oh, would I follow the whirlwind/ if only it would invite me." The translation, she thought, works on its own. But is it really a translation, or does it fall into the hybrid "variation" category?

Coining new words in order to fill lexical assymetries has been a widely used strategy among both translators and writers but has proven dangerous, and has frequently damaged more than helped the promotion of new indigenous written literature. Among average speakers of an Amerindian language, and given the fact that most of the adult indigenous population is now bilingual, whenever a subject is felt to be too difficult to be expressed in the native tongue, the speaker will typically use, depending on circumstances, Spanish, English, Portuguese or French, indulging in a to-and-fro dynamic between one language and another. Linguists call this phenomenon code switching. But code switching is also dangerous because it often sends the wrong signal to the younger generation, suggesting obsolescence of the native tongue. This, as well as the rejection of the hegemonic national language, has created a purist reaction among native writers and translators, who tend to fill lexical gaps from the source text to the translation with artificially constructed neologisms. By far the most widely used technique for creating these neologisms has been description by juxtaposition of roots, whenever languages allow this. Thus, a "pick-up" has become in the Tarahumara language (according to one such proposal) *"toame"*, which literally means "carrier." But since no description is ever sufficient (a "carrier" could also be a wheelbarrow or a suitcase), the resulting texts too often turn out to be cryptic and difficult to read. My recommendation would be to accept loans whenever they are in

common use, and introduce neologisms only when they are easy to understand and leave little room for ambiguity.

During the last five decades or so, economic, social and intellectual trends have deeply eroded the old, emotional loyalties toward ideas (and ideals) such as "people" or "nation," so prevalent during the Romantic and even modern eras, so the question nowadays is not why a writer should adopt one of the most widely spoken languages in the world as his or her tool of literary expression, but rather why *any* writer should cling to a language spoken only by tiny national minorities and within a very restricted geographical and social frame. Different answers can be given, ranging from emotional to rational, but the amazing fact is that literary production in these languages is a reality, and one that for the time being does not seem to be dwindling away or a passing trend.

When trying to emphasize the importance of preserving linguistic diversity, one must always remember, even if it sounds clichéd, that languages are not parallel systems of signs that "reflect" the world. Languages are, rather, independent—or at least *largely* independent—systems of interpretation of the world. And they are so because any set of words (nouns, adjectives, verbs) arbitrarily taxonomizes the world according to cultural synergies and values, as well as particular historical circumstances. Moreover, languages are living documents that encode much information about the communities that speak them, including historical facts not documented elsewhere. So whenever a language dies, mankind loses a real treasure chest of invaluable information and possibilities. Just one more reason to support the preservation and development of indigenous literatures.

I will end with yet another short poem, translated from the Tarahumara and written a couple of years ago by a young Tarahumara writer and translator, Martin Makawi:

> **Mapu ne bowichí inálo**
> **napisó pé napisó bí jú**
> **ba'wí pé ba'wí bí jú**
> **a'lí kó eeká pé eeká bí jú.**
> **Nóli bé mapua'lí we'érali ne awí**
> **a'lí kayaní napisó**
> **'Échi napisó ko**
> **kéti anayáwali sa'páala jú;**
> **'Échi ba'wí mápu 'mawá komíchi**
> **kéti Wichimóba lalá ju;**
> **A'lí eeká kó**
> **kéti retémali iwikáala jú.**

When I walk toward my village
the river's water is only water
dust is only dust
and wind
is nothing but wind.
But when I dance in the ceremonies
stirring up dust with my feet
rivers become the veins of this earth
dust my ancestors' flesh, and the wind
the spirit of my ancient people.

I believe the poem attests to the vigorous capacity of the indigenous languages of the Americas as vehicles of literary expression, bearing witness to both the particularities and the universals of human experience.

translating text, translating self

paulo da costa

Imagine me before a mirror, in conversation, in argument. I might be requesting clarification over the intent of a word or I may be arguing over the most accurate word to express my experience across two languages *face à face* in my mind. This image might elicit a suspicion of insanity for the unaware observer. On the other hand, for those of a more benevolent bent, it might appear as an act of ultimate contortion: brain yoga. This process carries its rewards and pitfalls. The back and forth shuttling of the languages inside my mind is not free from collisions and inadvertent collusions. The separateness is not achieved with ease. At times the mingling of words might prove beneficial.

Translating myself offers a second opportunity to strengthen the source text, a text that in itself already reflects an existing translation, the translation of my imagination and my emotions, of my thoughts and images into the medium of words.

The linguistic translation into either Portuguese or English, the second translation, establishes a feedback loop to that self who translated the world of my senses. It tests the effectiveness of the initial text in relation to its precision, it weighs the accuracy of its words, it sharpens the focus of its images. The translation reignites a dialogue and prompts me to return to my original text in order to polish an image or encourage the further ripening of a green thought. I return in order to sharpen the translation of my reasoning, of my senses and, in the end, deliver a creative work that is true to my intent. As a translator of my own work I am compelled to become a more attentive writer, challenged to improve my communication skills, and I gain a second pair of eyes with which to touch the page from a renewed perspective.

The process of translation unveils existing gaps in a source text; its inherent X-ray view of the edifice exposes, if existent, an inadequately built foundation or the hasty finishing-up touches in the house of words. There is no more attentive reader of an author's work than a translator's magnifying eye travelling with deliberate attention over the pages. This committed engagement begins with a sense of respectful responsibility: one who holds in his hand the voice of another and embraces the task of transporting that voice in its integrity to another context, another tongue. As a translator

I speak on behalf of another and therefore I must without doubt understand this other as I endeavour to deliver an effective translation. I must understand the varied implications of a single word; otherwise a paragraph may weigh on my shoulders and generate apprehension, if not paralyzing anxiety. Unburdened by such apprehensions, a leisurely reader may travel the landscape of a text without the weight of responsibility, perhaps such a reader even assumes the reading journey from his or her own presumed biases, a journey not unlike daily life filled with slips of misunderstanding. In the process of translating myself I enter a co-collaborative process of creation that affects and always transforms the source text. There is freedom and equality in this interaction. My attempt to understand and convey the original text elicits changes. Unlike the more common author-translator relationship that is unidirectional, my interactive experience travels a two-way street.

I believe there is an inherent acceptance that no translator can possibly speak on behalf of another without missing or adding variables to the equation of understanding: therefore approximation is a condition of engagement. This framework of acceptance propagates the tension and distance, caution and mistrust that remain embedded in the relationship. In translating myself, trust is inherent. I cannot betray myself without being aware of the trespass, and the weight of responsibility, the fear of not meeting expectations dissolves.

Since a translator must understand a writer in full to speak on their behalf, the task is condemned to fall short. Not because translators are particularly inept at understanding language, but because not even authors understand the whole range of possibilities contained in a text. That is the poetry of language, that is to say: the mystery. The resonance of our words is limitless. It is an echo without end, an echo that moves along the corridor of centuries and bounces in unique angles off the shifting texture of evolving cultures and shifting times. One cannot understand a person who fails to understand the sum of the self. And no person understands the self entirely. Perhaps living is a journey to discover the depths of who we are, breath by breath.

The dance of approximation expresses the condition of the engagement in translation; its shortcomings or the essence of its beauty depends on the outlook and expectations of the reader. If the impossibility of a complete meeting is accepted, then the dance of un-meeting becomes the essence of the experience. It is as it should be. I accept the impossibility of translating myself in full. As the words change shape and sound in the journey from one language to another, as the fluid ground shifts, the space between the call and response of the interaction embodies the essence I seek to create: a third entity. The marriage of the original text and translator, this marriage of two languages, will contain a piece of both, a piece adopting resemblances to the progenitors, yet unique in itself.

Translating myself offers an opportunity to strengthen the translation of self and become a more attentive and accomplished writer.

Translating Prose

beyondwords

Translating
the World

Comment se délester d'un trop-plein de théorie

André Gabastou

Littérature et traduction ont toujours suivi des voies parallèles, ce qui veut dire qu'elles coexistent mais ne se confondent pas. Toutefois, les phénomènes d'écho sont innombrables. L'apparition et l'évolution des genres littéraires ont été marquées par la traduction, c'est par exemple à partir d'elle que la France et l'Angleterre ont, au XVIIIe siècle, acclimaté le roman picaresque espagnol. À ce titre, le grand écrivain et traducteur barcelonais, Eduardo Mendoza déclarait, en 2006, aux rencontres sur la traduction littéraire de Tarazona : « Les grandes langues littéraires se sont formées par le biais des traductions. L'anglais est une langue qui surgit et se construit à partir de la Bible du roi Jacques, le russe littéraire commence à fonctionner quand Pouchkine traduit Shakespeare. » Il est donc faux de dire que les traducteurs se satisfont délibérément d'une pratique conventionnelle de l'écriture puisqu'ils sont souvent, qu'ils le veuillent ou non, à l'origine de ses mutations.

Si littérature et traduction avancent sans se confondre, on ne peut en dire autant du lexique qu'elles utilisent pour se décrire. On dit souvent d'un écrivain qu'il se traduit. Ce qui veut dire qu'à l'écoute de lui-même — de réminiscences, de rémanences, de souvenances, de souvenirs, de sensations et de manifestations de l'inconscient —, il tente de formuler en mots ce que sa rationalité a peine à comprendre. L'écrivain qui prête l'oreille à sa propre étrangeté entend souvent une langue qui lui est inconnue. Edgar Poe ignorait ce que signifiaient la vapeur blanchâtre dans laquelle baigne tout le paysage et l'étrange cri — tekeli-li — poussé à la fin des *Aventures d'Arthur Gordon Pym*. Et le texte, qu'on s'est pourtant efforcé d'interpréter, est aussi énigmatique pour nous qu'il l'était pour lui. Tout écrivain authentique affronte l'étrangeté de sa propre langue, mais il ne fait pas pour autant l'expérience de la langue de l'étranger, pratique propre au traducteur qui se cogne à une sphère dure, hermétique, qui lui résiste et le rejette, celle de la langue qui n'est pas la sienne et le renvoie à son altérité.

Le commerce des hommes, les échanges matériels et symboliques, les déplacements, les alliances et les affrontements font remonter la pratique de la traduction à une époque bien plus lointaine que celle de l'avènement de la littérature qui n'a commencé à exister en tant que telle qu'à l'orée des temps modernes. Par ailleurs la traduction n'est pas circonscrite par la littérature.

How to Jettison a Surfeit of Theory

André Gabastou

Literature and translation have always taken parallel
paths, co-existing yet never merging as one. However, the number of
echoing phenomena is countless. Both the arrival and evolution of
literary genres have been affected by translation. For instance, it was
through the auspices of translation that France and England adopted the
Spanish picaresque novel in the eighteenth century. In fact, well-known
Barcelona writer and translator Eduardo Mendoza stated at a symposium
in Tarazona in 2006 that, "The great literary languages have been shaped
by translation. English is a language that arose from and is founded on the
King James Bible, while Russian literature came into being with Pushkin's
translation of Shakespeare." It is false, then, to state that translators
deliberately practise conventional writing only since often, like it or
not, they are the source of writing's mutations.

While literature and translation move forward on parallel paths, the same
cannot be as easily claimed of the lexicon with which they describe themselves. It is often said that a writer translates him or herself. In other words,
by listening to himself—to reminiscences, remanence, remembering,
memories, sensations and manifestations of the unconscious—he tries to
express in words what his rational mind has trouble understanding. By connecting to his own strangeness, a writer often hears an unknown language.
Edgar Allen Poe had no idea of the meaning of the whitish vapour bathing
the landscape or of the strange cry – *tekeli-li* – at the end of *The Narrative of
Arthur Gordon Pym of Nantucket*. The text, despite repeated attempts at
interpretation, remains as enigmatic for us as it was for him. Any true
writer confronts the strangeness of his own language, yet the experience
does not bring him up against a foreign language in the same way as it
does a translator. The latter runs into a hard, hermetic sphere that resists
and rejects him, that of a language not his own which reminds him of
his otherness.

Commerce among people, material and symbolic exchanges, displace-
ments, alliances and confrontations necessitated translation long before
the emergence of literature, which only came into its present existence on
the cusp of modern times. Moreover, translation is not circumscribed by
literature.

La littérature et la traduction ont toujours fait l'objet de réflexions sans que celles-ci interfèrent forcément sur leur évolution. Mario Vargas Llosa a montré dans son ouvrage sur *Les Misérables* de Victor Hugo, *La Tentation de l'impossible*, combien le statut du narrateur était flou avant d'être défini par Flaubert dont *Madame Bovary* parut pourtant six ans avant *Les Misérables*. Avant Flaubert, il y avait une sorte d'« innocence du narrateur » qui pouvait occuper une place variable dans le récit sans qu'on y trouve à redire. Il en était de même pour la traduction. De la même manière qu'on a pu parler de photographie d'avant la photographie (celle-ci perd son innocence pour devenir un objet esthétique avec Man Ray, d'après Susan Sontag), on a pu parler de traduction d'avant la traduction. Il s'agissait de travaux naïfs, souvent menés par des aristocrates oisives qui se souciaient moins de fidélité que de conformité à leurs goûts et à leurs humeurs, modifiant les textes à leur gré, coupant des passages supposés trop longs, supprimant tel personnage fâcheux, en rajoutant tel autre. C'est ainsi que, dans notre adolescence, nous avons lu les grands Russes sans souffrir particulièrement des carences de la traduction. C'était le temps des « belles étrangères », des « belles infidèles », l'époque où traduire, c'était trahir, selon l'adage bien connu.

En s'attaquant à tous les phénomènes naturels et humains pour en faire des objets de science, on voit mal comment le positivisme aurait délaissé la langue et le langage appelés à devenir au fil des années les « sciences — au pluriel — du langage ». Savants et érudits se substitueraient à la figure frivole du traducteur dilettante et changeraient la nature de la traduction.

Dans cet ordre d'idées, le théoricien de la traduction Antoine Berman écrit dans *La Traduction et la lettre ou l'auberge du lointain* (1999) : « La traduction n'est ni une sous-littérature (comme l'a cru le XVIe siècle), ni une sous-critique (comme l'a cru le XIXe siècle). Elle n'est pas non plus une linguistique ou une poétique appliquée (comme on le croit au XXe siècle). La traduction est sujet et objet d'un savoir propre. Mais la traduction n'a (presque) jamais élevé son expérience au niveau d'une parole pleine et autonome, comme l'a fait (au moins depuis le Romantisme) la littérature. »

Elle l'a pourtant fait chez quelqu'un qui bouleversera comme on le verra ultérieurement une certaine conception de la traduction fondée sur l'imitation, éventuellement le pastiche et la parodie, dont Antoine Berman, décédé en 1991, ne pouvait qu'ignorer certains travaux décisifs : il s'agit d'Umberto Eco.

Literature and translation have always been the subject of reflection, without it necessarily having an impact on their evolution. Mario Vargas Llosa showed in his work on Victor Hugo's *Les Misérables, The Temptation of the Impossible*, how vague the narrator's status was until defined by Flaubert in *Madame Bovary*, albeit published six years before *Les Misérables*. Before Flaubert, there was a sort of "narrator's innocence" that could take up varying space in the tale without being criticized. The same held true for translation. Just as one could talk about photography before there was photography (which then lost its innocence when it became an aesthetic object with Man Ray, according to Susan Sontag), translation was spoken of before it existed. These were naïve attempts, often the work of aristocrats with time on their hands, less concerned with faithfulness than with bending the materials to their tastes and moods, changing texts at will, cutting supposedly over-lengthy passages, erasing annoying characters and adding others. That is how, in our adolescence, we read the great Russian authors without suffering particularly from the translations' failings. It was a time of "*belles étrangères*" and "*belles infidèles,*" a time when to translate was to betray, according to the well-known adage.

In making all natural and human phenomena a matter for scientific scrutiny, it is hard to see how positivism could have left out language and linguistics, which over time became "the language sciences" —in the plural. Academics and intellectuals replaced the frivolous and dilettante translators of the past and changed the nature of translation.

Along similar lines, translation theoretician Antoine Berman wrote in *La Traduction et la lettre ou L'auberge du lointain* (1999): "Translation is neither sub-literature (as was thought in the sixteenth century) or sub-criticism (as was thought in the nineteenth century). It is neither linguistics nor applied poetics (as was thought in the twentieth century). Translation is the subject and object of its own knowledge. But translation has (almost) never shown any will to raise itself to the same level of full autonomous discourse that literature has known (at least since Romanticism)."

It was, however, raised to that level in the work of one person, thus upsetting, as we shall see, a certain idea of translation as being based on imitation, possibly even pastiche and parody. Antoine Berman, who died in 1991, had no way of knowing of some of the decisive work being produced by Umberto Eco.

Le XIXe siècle, qui assiste au développement de la philologie, voit celle-ci s'étendre dans tout le champ linguistique : critique, établissement, datation des textes. La philologie se poste aux portes des grands classiques et en contrôle l'accès. Dépositaire de l'histoire des langues, il était normal, de par sa nature, qu'elle procède à des traductions visant à restituer le sens des œuvres. Étrangère aux catégories esthétiques, elle « serre les textes au plus près » en s'appuyant sur son savoir linguistique et sa connaissance des langues. Ce faisant, elle discrédite tout autre manière de traduire (celle des créateurs, Nerval, Valéry, Gide, respectée mais jugée trop subjective et celle des praticiens de la traduction qui, lorsqu'ils ne sont pas universitaires, sont tenus pour des amateurs). En jouant la littéralité contre la lettre, comme dirait Antoine Berman, la traduction philologique produit parfois des objets littéraires archaïsants qui ont laissé des générations perplexes telle la traduction de la *Divine comédie* de Dante par André Pézard qui fit autorité jusqu'à la reprise en main du texte par Jacqueline Risset.

Antoine Berman perçoit l'apport de la philologie à la pratique de la traduction (une exigence de précision) et ses limites (l'évitement de la lettre, la traduction perdant son statut d'œuvre d'art pour devenir l'apanage des universitaires), mais il sous-estime, peut-être pour des raisons chronologiques, ce sur quoi repose désormais toute réflexion sur la traduction : on sait, au moins depuis Jakobson, que l'équivalence linguistique n'existe pas. Tel est le point de départ de la réflexion d'Umberto Eco dans les divers essais sur la traduction réunis en un seul volume intitulé *Dire presque la même chose — Expériences de traduction* (2006). On en conseillera vivement la lecture à tout jeune traducteur car elle le libérera du carcan dans lequel on a enfermé la traduction : le texte traduit doit être fidèle à l'original. La langue A n'étant pas la langue B, la traduction dans la langue B du texte écrit dans la langue A n'en est pas l'équivalent, mais la métaphore, d'où le « presque la même chose ». L'enjeu est considérable, tous les critères de jugement subissent une profonde mutation et obligent à lire autrement les traductions. Comment faut-il procéder si l'on tient compte de ce que dit Umberto Eco ? Le traducteur de *Sylvie* de Nerval et des *Exercices de style* de Queneau en italien donne un premier élément de réponse : « Au cours de mes expériences d'auteur traduit, j'étais sans cesse déchiré entre le besoin que la version soit « fidèle » à ce que j'avais écrit et la découverte excitante de la façon dont mon texte pouvait (et même parfois *devait*) se transformer au moment où il était redit dans une autre langue ». Plus loin, il ajoute : « ... le concept de fidélité participe de la conviction que la traduction est une des formes de l'interprétation et qu'elle doit toujours viser, fût-ce en partant de la sensibilité et de la culture du

The nineteenth century saw the development of philology and its spread to the linguistic domain: the criticism, establishment and dating of texts. Philology is posted at the doors of the great classics and controls any access thereto. As the storehouse for the history of languages, its very nature dictated that it should proceed with translations designed to restitute the meaning of the great works. Foreign to aesthetic categories, it "followed the texts as closely as possible," shored up by its linguistic know-how and knowledge of languages. In doing so, it discredited all other ways of translating (that of creators such as Nerval, Valéry and Gide, though respected, was deemed too subjective, and that of translation practitioners who, when not academics, were seen as amateurs). By playing literality against literature, as Antoine Berman would say, philological translation sometimes produced archaic-sounding literary objects that left later generations confused, such as André Pézard's translation of Dante's *La Divina Commedia*, which was seen as the last word on the subject until Jacqueline Risset provided a new translation.

Antoine Berman understands philology's contribution to the practice of translation (the requirement for precision) and its limits (by ignoring the purely literary, translation loses its status as a work of art and becomes nothing more than a playing field for academics). However, he underestimates, possibly for chronological reasons, what was to serve as a base for all future reflection on the act of translation. We know, at least since Jakobson, that linguistic equivalence does not exist. This is the starting point for Umberto Eco's meditations in his various essays on translation brought together in a single volume entitled *Saying Almost the Same Thing: Experiences in Translation* (2006). All young translators should read this and be free of the shackles restraining translation, namely that the translated text must be faithful to the original. Since language A is not Language B, the translation in Language B of a written text in language A is not its equivalent, but rather a metaphor, or "almost the same thing." The stakes are high: all criteria for judgment are radically changed and necessitate another look at translation. How to proceed if we take Umberto Eco into account? The Italian translator of Nerval's *Sylvie* and Queneau's *Exercices de style* provides a partial answer: "Over the course of my experience as a translated author, I have always been torn between the need for a "faithful" version of what I'd written and the exciting discovery of how my text could (and sometimes must) change on becoming its re-expression in another language." Further on, he adds, " . . . the concept of faithfulness comes from the conviction that translation is a form of interpretation and must always try to find, albeit starting from the reader's sensibility and

lecteur, à retrouver je ne dis pas l'intention de l'auteur, mais *l'intention du texte*, ce que le texte dit ou suggère en rapport avec la langue dans laquelle il est exprimé et au contexte culturel où il est né ». Dans « La tâche du traducteur », qui date de 1923, Walter Benjamin disait déjà quelque chose de semblable : « Une traduction qui rend fidèlement chaque mot ne peut presque jamais restituer pleinement le sens qu'a le mot dans l'original ».

Au cours d'une conférence que j'ai prononcée l'année dernière à l'École normale supérieure, j'ai expliqué combien la traduction d'une œuvre majeure de l'Argentin Alan Pauls, *Le Passé*, m'avait laissé en un premier temps perplexe, car je n'arrivais pas à voir ce qui en faisait un objet littéraire. Ce n'était ni la temporalité ni l'espace ni la situation ni les personnages. Un jour, plongé dans *En lisant, en écrivant* de Julien Gracq, j'ai eu une sorte de révélation lorsque je suis tombé sur cette phrase : « Il y a pour chaque époque de l'art un rythme intime, aussi naturel, aussi spontané chez elle que peut l'être le rythme de la respiration, et qui, beaucoup plus profondément que son pittoresque extérieur, plus profondément même que les images-clés qui la hantent, la met en prise sur l'être et réellement la fait exister : c'est à ce rythme seulement que le monde pour elle se met à danser en mesure, c'est à cette allure seule qu'elle capte et traduit la vie, tout comme l'aiguille du gramophone ne peut lire un disque qu'à une certaine vitesse réglée et fixe ».

La lecture libératrice de cette phrase m'a arraché au bourbier dans lequel je m'enlisais. Prisonnier du titre du roman et du système de subordination proustien, je n'arrivais pas à en détacher le phrasé de Pauls. Mais j'ai à ce moment-là compris que d'une certaine manière l'écriture de Pauls était aux antipodes de celle de Proust : les mots y sont toujours happés par un futur que rien ne préfigure et ce mouvement donne une accélération inouïe au récit. Ils l'emballent littéralement.

J'étais, au départ, moins égaré dans le roman du Salvadorien Horacio Castellanos Moya, *Donde no estén ustedes, Là où vous ne serez pas* (2008). D'abord parce qu'il ne renvoie à aucun titre français, ensuite parce que j'avais déjà traduit l'un de ses romans, *La diabla en el espejo, La Mort d'Olga María* (2004) et je m'étais familiarisé avec son traitement particulier des voix et, pour finir, j'avais travaillé avec lui au cours d'un séjour au Banff Centre (Alberta, Canada) où nous avions bénéficié d'une bourse en juin 2007 grâce à l'entremise de Brigitte Bouchard, directrice de la maison d'édition qui publie l'auteur à Montréal.

culture, I won't say the author's intention, but the *text's intention*, what the text states or suggests in relation to the language in which it is expressed and the cultural context in which it took shape." In "The Task of the Translator" published in 1923, Walter Benjamin already held a similar view: "A translation that faithfully renders each word almost never fully restitutes the meaning of the original."

During a conference I gave last year at the École normale supérieure, I explained how much the translation of a major work by the Argentine writer Alan Pauls, *Le Passé* [The Past], at first flummoxed me because I could not see what made it a literary text. It was not its temporality or the place or situation or characters. One day, reading Julien Gracq's *En lisant, en écrivant*, I had a revelation when I came upon the following: "For each period of art, there is an intimate rhythm, as natural and spontaneous as the rhythm of the breath that, much more than the picturesque exterior, more deeply than the key images haunting it, allows it to take hold of being and brings it to life: only at that rhythm does its world dance in time, only at that pace is its life captured and translated, just as the gramophone's needle can only read a record at a given speed."

The liberating pull of that sentence freed me from the quagmire in which I had been struggling. Imprisoned by the novel's title and the Proustian system of subordination, I had had trouble identifying Pauls' phrasing. But at that precise moment, I understood that, in a certain fashion, Pauls' writing was the exact opposite of Proust's: words continually collide with a future that nothing can forecast and the ensuing movement gives the tale incredible impetus. It literally carries it away.

I was not as lost initially in the novel by Salvadoran writer Horacio Castellanos Moya, *Donde no estén ustedes* (*Là où vous ne serez pas*, 2008). First, because it makes no allusion to a French title; second, because I had already translated one of his novels, *La diabla en el espejo* (*La Mort d'Olga María*, 2004) and had become familiar with his particular approach to voice; and, finally, because I was able to work with him during a residency in June of 2007 at The Banff Centre in Alberta, Canada thanks to a grant made possible by the good offices of Brigitte Bouchard, director of his Quebec publisher in Montreal.

Né en 1957, Horacio Castellanos Moya a quitté le Salvador après avoir été menacé de mort pour avoir publié un livre d'une grande violence sur son pays, *El asco, Thomas Berhnard en San Salvador, Le Dégoût* (2003). Son œuvre est aujourd'hui traduite et publiée régulièrement par les Allusifs au rythme d'un roman par an.

Donde no estén ustedes, Là où vous ne serez pas, est composé de deux parties. Dans la première, « L'effondrement », après un voyage chaotique, Alberto Aragón, ancien ambassadeur du Salvador au Nicaragua, vieux beau alcoolique dont une jeune Mexicaine, l'Infante, s'est éprise, arrive par un matin de juin 1994 dans la capitale du District Fédéral pour s'y confronter à sa dernière aventure : une lente descente vers les ténèbres. Ayant toujours nagé en eaux troubles, il est abandonné par ses anciens amis et mourra ruiné dans une sordide chambre de bonne située sur un toit en terrasse de Mexico. Dans la seconde partie, « L'Enquête », un privé salvadorien, José Pindonga, qu'on connaît depuis *La Mort d'Olga María,* est chargé par un vieil ami de l'ambassadeur d'élucider les circonstances mystérieuses de sa mort et le roman se termine par un épilogue qui déjoue toutes les hypothèses du lecteur. Roman historique et politique (la guerre civile au Salvador, les forces en présence, les enjeux de pouvoir et d'argent), roman policier (comment est mort Alberto Aragón ?), roman d'amours tronquées, roman existentiel (des vies fracassées), *Là où vous ne serez pas* est tout cela et bien plus encore. Construit en deux blocs symétriques et antithétiques, une première partie qui est une lente descente aux enfers et une seconde dans laquelle s'entrecroisent un certain nombre de personnages hystériques, *Là où vous ne serez pas* décrit les deux faces d'un même destin, Pindonga étant le double existentiel de l'ambassadeur Aragón. Ce qui pose problème au traducteur, c'est moins la langue d'Horacio Castellanos Moya qui refuse toute inscription vernaculaire que les deux voix narratives du roman : dans la première partie, un narrateur omniscient raconte les derniers jours de l'ambassadeur Alberto Aragón ; dans la seconde, un Pindonga décati et vibrionnant, obsédé sexuel, d'une vulgarité extrême, mène l'enquête. Récit contre oralité, marche forcée contre frénésie, gravité contre hystérie. Telle est la lettre du roman, la grosse caisse de la marche funèbre s'opposant à la crécelle pindonguienne qui rythme des chapitres d'une seule phrase.

Première partie.

« **Tirado en el pequeño camastro, exhausto, con la ropa arrugada y barba de dos días, Alberto Aragón ha visto entrar a la Infanta, gordita, mofletuda, con los pantalones holgados y la chaqueta de mezclilla azul, la gordita que sólo empujó la puerta de esa habitación de azotea, esa cueva para servidumbre a la que**

Born in 1957, Horacio Castellanos Moya left El Salvador after receiving death threats for publishing a powerful critical assault on his country, *El asco, Thomas Bernard en San Salvador* (*Le Dégoût*, 2003). His work is being translated and published by Les Allusifs at the rate of one novel per year.

Donde no estén ustedes (Là où vous ne serez pas) is divided into two parts. In the first part, "The Collapse," after a chaotic trip, Alberto Aragón, former Salvadoran ambassador to Nicaragua, a good-looking elderly alcoholic who is loved by a young Mexican woman, l'Infante, arrives one morning in June 1994 in Mexico City to face his last adventure: a gradual descent into darkness. Having made the most of troubled waters, he has been abandoned by his former friends and will die penniless in a sordid maid's room on a rooftop in Mexico. In the second part, "The Investigation," a Salvadoran private eye, José Pindonga, who first appeared in *La diabla en el espejo*, is asked by an old friend of the ambassador to clear up the mysterious circumstances around his death, and the novel concludes with an epilogue that confounds all the reader's expectations. A historical and political novel (the civil war in El Salvador, the authority in power, the stakes of power and money), a detective novel (how did Alberto Aragón die?), a novel of love cut short, an existential novel (around broken lives), *Donde no estén ustedes* is all that and more. Structured as two symmetrical and antithetical blocks, a Part 1 that is a slow descent into hell and a Part 2 that introduces several hysterical characters and their encounters, *Donde no estén ustedes* describes the two faces of a single destiny, with Pindonga as an existential double for Ambassador Aragón. The problem for the translator is not so much that Horacio Castellanos Moya's language rejects any vernacular register but that the novel has two narrative voices: in Part 1, an omniscient narrator relates Ambassador Alberto Aragón's last days; in Part 2, a decrepit, nerve-wracked and sexually obsessed Pindonga is in charge of the investigation. It is a tale of written vs. oral culture, a forced march against frenzy, gravity against hysteria. Such is the literary nature of the novel, a bass drum in the funeral march in stark contrast to the Pindonguian rattle that punctuates the single-sentence chapters.

Part One.

Tirado en el pequeño camastro, exhausto, con la ropa arrugada y barba de dos días, Alberto Aragón ha visto entrar a la Infanta, gordita, mofletuda, con los pantalones holgados y la chaqueta de mezclilla azul, la gordita que sólo empujó la puerta de esa habitación de azotea, esa cueva para servidumbre a la que

recién lo ha llevado, esa ratonera en la que ahora se apretuja Alberto Aragón sobre el pequeño camastro, rodeado de cajas que, con sus pocas pertenencias, en tan minúsculo espacio parecen llenarlo todo. »

Allitérations (en o et a), répétitions, rythme processionnaire, le ton est donné dès le départ.

« Étendu sur le petit grabat, à bout de forces, vêtements froissés et barbe de deux jours, Alberto Aragón a vu entrer l'Infante, grassouillette, joufflue, pantalon ample et veste en toile de jean, la grassouillette qui s'est contentée de pousser la porte de cette chambre donnant sur une terrasse, cette grotte pour domestiques où elle vient de l'emmener, ce piège à rats où Alberto Aragón se pelotonne sur le petit grabat, entouré de caisses qui semblent, avec ses maigres biens, occuper entièrement un espace aussi exigu. »

Deuxième partie.

« La noche del viernes me abstuve de ir a El Balcón, aunque me moría de ganas de visitar mi bar-café favorito, de mostrar mi boleto de avión y de contar mis planes en México ante la admiración de la muchachada femenil, creí inconveniente arriesgarme a caer en la tentación de una sola copa que hubiera sido capaz de echar por tierra mi esplenderosa entrada a un nuevo empleo y a una nueva vida, mi temor a estropear la cara feliz con que el destino comenzaba a tratarme fue tal que me propuse pasar esa noche de viernes en casa, sin hacer otra cosa que estar tirado frente a la vieja tele blanco y negro, pero sin poner atención a las estupideces de los programas que estaban al aire, sino pensando en esas dos ideas que comenzaban a meterse obsesivamente en mi cabeza, la primera de las cuales era que detrás de la voluntad de Jeremy Irons de investigar la muerte del ex embajador Alberto Aragón había un motivo oculto que no sería fácil descubrir, un motivo que probablemente sólo conocían mi cliente y el finado, y la segunda idea era que los kilos de mortificación con que me había intoxicado a causa del abandono de Rita Mena estaban relacionados con el hecho de que yo era quince años mayor que ella... »

Phrase interminable, digressions, subordinations et concessions empilées, répétitions, jacassement, rhétorique de la logorrhée et du remplissage.

« Dans la soirée du vendredi, je me suis abstenu d'aller au Balcón, même si je mourais d'envie d'aller faire un tour dans mon bar préféré, de montrer mon billet d'avion et de raconter mes projets à Mexico sous les yeux admiratifs de la bande de femmes, j'ai pensé qu'il n'était pas convenable de me laisser tenter par un seul verre qui aurait été capable de mettre en pièces mes splendides débuts dans un nouvel emploi et une nouvelle vie, ma crainte d'ébranler le tour heureux pris par mon destin était telle que je me suis proposé de passer la nuit du vendredi à la maison, couché devant le vieux téléviseur en noir et blanc, mais sans faire attention aux stupidités des émissions à la mode,

recién lo ha llevado, esa ratonera en la que ahora se apretuja Alberto Aragón sobre el pequeño camastro, rodeado de cajas que, con sus pocas pertenencias, en tan minúsculo espacio parecen llenarlo todo.»

With its use of alliteration (final o and a), repetition and a processional rhythm, the tone is given from the outset.

« Étendu sur le petit grabat, à bout de forces, vêtements froissés et barbe de deux jours, Alberto Aragón a vu entrer l'Infante, grassouillette, joufflue, pantalon ample et veste en toile de jean, la grassouillette qui s'est contentée de pousser la porte de cette chambre donnant sur une terrasse, cette grotte pour domestiques où elle vient de l'emmener, ce piège à rats où Alberto Aragón se pelotonne sur le petit grabat, entouré de caisses qui semblent, avec ses maigres biens, occuper entièrement un espace aussi exigu.»

Part Two.

« La noche del viernes me abstuve de ir a El Balcón, aunque me moría de ganas de visitar mi bar-café favorito, de mostrar mi boleto de avión y de contar mis planes en México ante la admiración de la muchachada femenil, creí inconveniente arriesgarme a caer en la tentación de une sola copa que hubiera sido capaz de echar por tierra mi esplenderosa entrada a un nuevo empleo y a una nueva vida, mi temor a estropear la cara feliz con que el destino comenzaba a tratarme fue tal que me propuse pasar esa noche de viernes en casa, sin hacer otra cosa que estar tirado frente a la vieja tele blanco y negro, pero sin poner atención a las estupideces de los programas que estaban al aire, sino pensando en esas dos ideas que comenzaban a meterse obsesivamente en mi cabeza, la primera de las cuales era que detrás de la voluntad de Jeremy Irons de investigar la muerte del ex embajador Alberto Aragón había un motivo oculto que no sería fácil descubrir, un motivo que probablemente sólo conocían mi cliente y el finado, y la segunda idea era que los kilos de mortificación con que me había intoxicado a causa del abandono de Rita Mena estaban relacionados con el hecho de que yo era quince años mayor que ella...»

The run-on sentence, the exaggerated use of digressions, subordination and concessions, repetition, chatter, a rhetorical style replete with logorrhea and filler.

« Dans la soirée du vendredi, je me suis abstenu d'aller au Balcón, même si je mourais d'envie d'aller faire un tour dans mon bar préféré, de montrer mon billet d'avion et de raconter mes projets à Mexico sous les yeux admiratifs de la bande de femmes, j'ai pensé qu'il n'était pas convenable de me laisser tenter par un seul verre qui aurait été capable de mettre en pièces mes splendides débuts dans un nouvel emploi et une nouvelle vie, ma crainte d'ébranler le tour heureux pris par mon destin était telle que je me suis proposé de passer la nuit du vendredi à la maison, couché devant le vieux téléviseur en noir et blanc, mais sans faire attention aux stupidités des émissions à la mode,

uniquement pour penser à deux idées qui commençaient à m'obséder,
la première étant que, derrière la volonté de Jeremy Irons d'enquêter sur la
mort de l'ex-ambassadeur Alberto Aragón, il y avait une raison cachée difficile
à découvrir, une raison que ne connaissaient probablement que mon client et le
défunt, la seconde que les kilos de mortification avec lesquels je m'étais intoxi-
qué à cause de l'abandon de Rita Mena étaient liés aux quinze ans que
j'avais de plus qu'elle... »

Mettre en regard le texte premier et le texte second montre, en creux,
ce qui menace tout travail de traduction : la surtraduction. Surtraduire
donne un tour de vis sans nécessité à cette interprétation qu'est toute
traduction (Heidegger) et la fait dériver vers le pastiche, autrement dit
le grotesque. Une écoute attentive du texte premier et du texte second
fera sans doute dire que traduction philologique et traduction au sens où
l'entend Umberto Eco donnent en définitive des résultats assez proches,
ce qui est vrai, à cela près que seule la seconde manière de traduire permet
de dépasser la texture de l'original pour en inventer une autre en perdant
de vue l'impératif de la fidélité et la comptabilité absurde de la perte et du
gain. Comme l'a longuement expliqué l'écrivain basque Bernardo Atxaga
qui a autant traduit qu'écrit puisqu'il écrit en basque puis se traduit
lui-même en espagnol : le traducteur et le lecteur ne pouvant évaluer avec
exactitude ce qui se perd et se gagne dans une traduction, la question
relève de la métaphysique.

Pour mettre un terme à ce problème aussi vain qu'inutile, citons une
figure emblématique de la traduction latino-américaine, Jorge Luis Borges
: « Présupposer que toute recombinaison d'éléments est obligatoirement
inférieure à son original revient à présupposer que le brouillon 9 est
obligatoirement inférieur au brouillon H — car il ne peut y avoir que des
brouillons. L'idée de " texte définitif " ne relève que de la religion ou de
la fatigue. »

uniquement pour penser à deux idées qui commençaient à m'obséder,
la première étant que, derrière la volonté de Jeremy Irons d'enquêter sur la
mort de l'ex-ambassadeur Alberto Aragón, il y avait une raison cachée difficile
à découvrir, une raison que ne connaissaient probablement que mon client et le
défunt, la seconde que les kilos de mortification avec lesquels je m'étais intoxi-
qué à cause de l'abandon de Rita Mena étaient liés aux quinze ans que
j'avais de plus qu'elle... »

A comparison of text one and text two shows what most threatens any
translation endeavour: overtranslation. Overtranslation is a needless tight-
ening of the screw in the interpretation that constitutes any translation
(Heidegger), making it veer towards pastiche, i.e. the grotesque. A close
reading aloud of the first and second texts will have some undoubtedly
saying that, in the final analysis, philological translation and translation for
sense as described by Umberto Eco lead to similar results, which is true,
except that only the second approach makes it possible to go beyond the
texture of the original to invent another texture by ignoring the requirement of faithfulness and the absurd exercise of chalking up gains and
losses. As was explained at length by Basque writer Bernardo Atxaga, who
has translated as much as he has written since he writes in Basque and
translates himself into Spanish, translators and readers cannot evaluate
with precision what is lost and what is gained in a translation, and
thus the issue itself is metaphysical.

To have done once and for all with an issue as pointless as it is useless,
let us listen to an emblematic figure in Latin-American translation,
Jorge Luis Borges: "To assume that any recombination of elements is
bound to be inferior to the original is akin to assuming that draft 9 is
bound to be inferior to draft H—since drafts are all that are possible.
The idea of a 'definitive text' comes only from either religion
or exhaustion."

Translation by S. Ouriou

Translating Don Quixote

Edith Grossman

In the author's prologue to what is now called part I of
Don Quixote (part II appeared ten years later, in 1615, following the
publication of a continuation of the knight's adventures written by
someone using the pseudonym "Avellaneda"), Cervantes said this
about his book and the need to write a preface for it:

> I wanted only to offer it to you plain and bare, unadorned by a prologue or the
> endless catalogue of sonnets, epigrams, and laudatory poems that are usually
> placed at the beginning of books. For I can tell you that although it cost me
> some effort to compose, none seemed greater than creating the preface you are
> now reading. I picked up my pen many times to write it, and many times I put it
> down again because I did not know what to write; and once, when I was baffled,
> with the paper in front of me, my pen behind my ear, my elbow propped on
> the writing table and my cheek resting in my hand, pondering what I would say,
> a friend of mine ... came in, and seeing me so perplexed he asked the reason,
> and I ... said I was thinking about the prologue I had to write for the history
> of Don Quixote....

Cervantes's fictional difficulty was certainly my factual one as I contemplat-
ed the prospect of writing even a few lines about the wonderfully utopian
task of translating the first—and probably the greatest—modern novel.
Substitute keyboard and monitor for pen and paper, and my dilemma and
posture were the same; the dear friend who helped me solve the problem
was really Cervantes himself, an embodied spirit who emerged out of the
shadows and off the pages when I realized I could begin this note by
quoting a few sentences from his prologue.

I call the undertaking utopian in the sense intended by Ortega y Gasset
when he deemed translations utopian but then went on to say that all
human efforts to communicate—even in the same language—are equally
utopian, equally luminous with value, and equally worth the doing.
Endeavoring to translate artful writing, particularly an indispensable work
like *Don Quixote*, grows out of infinite optimism as the translator valiantly,
perhaps quixotically, attempts to enter the mind of the first writer through
the gateway of the text. It is a daunting and inspiring enterprise.

I have never kept a translating journal, though I admire those I have read.
Keeping records of any kind is not something I do easily, and after six or

seven hours of translating at the computer, the idea of writing about what I have written looms insurmountably, as does the kind of self-scrutiny required: the actuality of the translation is in the translation, and having to articulate how and why I have just articulated the text seems cruelly redundant. Yet there are some general considerations that may be of interest to you. I hesitated over the spelling of the protagonist's name, for instance, and finally opted for an x, not a j, in Quixote (I wanted the connection to the English "quixotic" to be immediately apparent); I debated the question of footnotes with myself and decided I was obliged to put some in, though I had never used them before in a translation (I did not want the reader to be put off by references that may now be obscure, or to miss the layers of intention and meaning those allusions create); I wondered about consulting other translations and vowed not to—at least in the beginning—in order to keep my ear clear and the voice of the translation free of outside influences (I kept the vow for the first year, and then, from time to time, I glanced at other people's work); I chose to use Martin de Riquer's edition of *Don Quixote*, which is based on the first printing of the book (with all its historic slips and errors) and has useful notes that include discussions of problematic words and phrases based on Riquer's comparisons of the earliest seventeenth-century translations into English, French, and Italian. Finally, I assure you that I felt an ongoing, unstoppable rush of exhilaration and terror, for perfectly predictable and transparent reasons, at undertaking so huge and so important a project.

Every translator has to live with the kind of pedantic critic who is always ready to pounce at an infelicitous phrase or misinterpreted word in a book that can be hundreds of pages long. I had two or three soul-searing nightmares about rampaging hordes laying waste to my translation of the work that is not only the great monument of literature in Spanish but a pillar of the entire Western literary tradition. The extraordinary significance and influence of this novel were reaffirmed, once again, in 2002, when one hundred major writers from fifty-four countries voted *Don Quixote* the best work of fiction in the world. One reason for the exalted position it occupies is that Cervantes's book contains within itself, in germ or full-blown, practically every imaginative technique and device used by subsequent fiction writers to engage their readers and construct their works. The prospect of translating it was stupefying.

Shortly before I began work, while I was wrestling with the question of what kind of voice would be most appropriate for the translation of a book written some four hundred years ago, 1 mentioned my fears to Julian Ríos,

the Spanish novelist. His reply was simple and profound and immensely liberating. He told me not to be afraid; Cervantes, he said, was our most modern writer, and what I had to do was to translate him the way I translated everyone else—that is, the contemporary authors whose works I have brought over into English. Julian's characterization was a revelation; it desacralized the project and allowed me, finally, to confront the text and find the voice in English. For me this is the essential challenge in translation: hearing, in the most profound way I can, the text in Spanish and discovering the voice to say (I mean, to write) the text again in English. Compared to that, lexical difficulties shrink and wither away.

I believe that my primary obligation as a literary translator is to re-create for the reader in English the experience of the reader in Spanish. When Cervantes wrote *Don Quixote*, it was not yet a seminal masterpiece of European literature, the book that crystallized forever the making of literature out of life and literature, that explored in typically ironic fashion, and for the first time, the blurred and shifting frontiers between fact and fiction, imagination and history, perception and physical reality, or that set the stage for all Hispanic studies and all serious discussions of the history and nature of the novel. When Cervantes wrote *Don Quixote*, his language was not archaic or quaint. He wrote in a crackling, up-to-date Spanish that was an intrinsic part of his time (this is instantly apparent when he has Don Quixote, in transports of knightly madness, speak in the old-fashioned idiom of the novels of chivalry), a modern language that both reflected and helped to shape the way people experienced the world. This meant that I did not need to find a special, anachronistic, somehow-seventeenth-century voice but could translate his astonishingly fine writing into contemporary English.

And his writing is a marvel: it gives off sparks and flows like honey. Cervantes's style is so artful it seems absolutely natural and inevitable; his irony is sweet-natured, his sensibility sophisticated, compassionate, and humorous. If my translation works at all, the reader should keep turning the pages, smiling a good deal, periodically bursting into laughter, and impatiently waiting for the next synonym (Cervantes delighted in accumulating synonyms, especially descriptive ones, within the same phrase), the next mind-bending coincidence, the next variation on the structure of

Don Quixote's adventures, the next incomparable conversation between the knight and his squire. To quote again from Cervantes's prologue: "I do not want to charge you too much for the service I have performed in introducing you to so noble and honorable a knight; but I do want you to thank me for allowing you to make the acquaintance of the famous Sancho Panza, his squire...."

I began the work in February 2001 and completed it two years later, but it is important for you to know that "final" versions are determined more by a publisher's due date than by any sense on my part that the work is actually finished. Even so, I hope you find it deeply amusing and truly compelling. If not, you can be certain the fault is mine.

Traduction: Musique, Éthique

Hélène Rioux

Quand on aborde le sujet de la traduction littéraire, une
question revient immanquablement : Traduire, trahir ? Comme s'il n'y
avait que cette question. Comme si le débat ne pouvait tourner qu'autour
de ce choix fondamental. Comme si la traduction n'était finalement
qu'une affaire de loyauté ou de trahison. Comme si le traducteur était toujours placé devant cette éventualité terrifiante : se transformer en traître.

Vu sous cet angle, un problème d'éthique, à tout le moins d'éthique
professionnelle, semble se poser d'entrée de jeu. C'est le premier qui se
pose au traducteur digne de ce nom. « Parviendrai-je à rendre la pensée
de l'autre dans son intégralité, à donner toutes les nuances de ses images,
toute la musicalité de sa langue ? Lui rendrai-je justice ? »

«Est-ce que je crois à cette œuvre ? se demande-t-il aussi. En acceptant de
la traduire, suis-je loyal envers mes convictions intimes, ma foi, ma propre
vision de la vie ?» Traduire l'autre en lui étant fidèle, sans se trahir
soi-même : voilà où réside le défi.

Je suis tombée des nues la première fois que j'ai pris conscience du
dilemme qui hante certains traducteurs — et leurs critiques, puristes
mélancoliques qui, dans leur quête effrénée de l'«authentique», déplorent
toujours de n'avoir pas accès à l'œuvre originale, qui considèrent sa traduction comme un sous-produit, un ersatz, qui refusent de voir la part
— essentielle — de création qui entre dans une traduction ou d'y accorder
la moindre importance — sauf quand il s'agit de la prendre en faute —,
qui refusent de penser que la traduction puisse enrichir — ô blasphème !
— l'original. Car, pour eux, l'œuvre originale est une chose statique, im-
muable, coulée dans le béton, figée dans le temps et l'espace, une chose
que toute manipulation ne peut que profaner, corrompre. Je parle de ceux
pour qui tous les traducteurs sont malhonnêtes — pour ainsi dire, des
faussaires —, toute traduction est un crime — pour ainsi dire, une contre-
façon. C'est du moins ce que, avec une hargne qui me semble injustifiée,
Jules Renard a écrit dans son Journal. Je dis «injustifiée» car, enfin, si, comme lui, je frémis d'horreur devant la médiocrité de certaines traductions,
j'éprouve pourtant de véritables frissons de bonheur admiratif devant
l'excellence de certaines autres. (Remarquons que l'horreur vient surtout
quand il s'agit de poésie, musique d'une langue à l'état pur, son âme, en
quelque sorte. Cette musique particulière de la langue, cette âme,

Translation: Music, Ethics

Hélène Rioux

The subject of literary translation inevitably raises the question: translation or treason? As though there were only one question. As though the discussion could focus only on this one fundamental choice. As though translation were, in the final analysis, nothing but a question of fidelity or betrayal. As though the translator were forever confronted with the terrifying possibility of becoming a traitor.

From this perspective, an ethical issue, or at least an issue of professional ethics, seems to emerge at the outset. It is the first question any translator worthy of the title asks him- or herself. "Will I be able to convey another's thoughts fully, providing all the nuances of the author's images and all the musicality of the author's language? Will I do the author's work justice?"

The next question a translator might ask is, "Do I believe in this work? By agreeing to translate it, am I being true to my profound convictions, my faith, my own world view?" The challenge being to translate another while remaining loyal both to that author and one's own self.

I had trouble believing such a dilemma haunts certain translators—and their critics, melancholy purists who, in their frantic quest for "authenticity," forever bemoan the lack of access to the original. They consider translation as a byproduct, an ersatz text, and refuse either to acknowledge the crucial part of creation that must enter into any translation or to grant it any importance—except to criticize—and refuse to believe that translation might even enrich—such blasphemy! —the original. For them, the original work is a static, immutable object cast in stone, frozen in time and space, an object that can only be profaned, corrupted by any manipulation. I am speaking of those reviewers who see all translators as dishonest—counterfeiters, as it were—and all translation as a crime—counterfeit, as it were. At least those were Jules Renard's words in his Journal, delivered with what I see as undeserved ferocity. I say "undeserved" because, even though, like him, I shudder in horror at the mediocrity of certain translations, on the other hand, I experience a genuine thrill of admiration at the excellence of others. (Note that the horror comes most often with poetry, the music of language in its pure state, its soul in a way. A language's particular music,

serait-elle intraduisible — intransmissible ? On dit aussi que la poésie est ce qui, inévitablement et irrémédiablement, se perd dans la traduction. Mais si la poésie de l'auteur est perdue, celle du traducteur ne pourrait-elle prendre le relais ?)

Traduire, trahir... Les deux mots se ressemblent, et c'était facile de faire le rapprochement. Trop facile, peut-être. Si je suis tombée des nues, c'est que je n'avais jamais regardé la traduction selon un point de vue aussi mani-chéen. Je la voyais plutôt comme une entreprise généreuse, une sorte de mission, visant à propager la bonne nouvelle — la bonne littérature. Une entreprise désintéressée, car les sommes d'argent en jeu sont, la plupart du temps, dérisoires par rapport au travail accompli, et la gloire, inutile même d'en parler.

Dans mon cas, s'il faut parler de la genèse, tout a commencé par le désir, l'urgence de dire. Dès l'enfance, une foule d'émotions semblaient se bousculer à l'intérieur de moi, qui voulaient émerger à l'air libre. Les livres m'ont d'emblée tenu compagnie, m'ont enchantée. Ils me parlaient, je m'identifiais aux personnages, leurs combats, leurs tourments devenaient les miens — d'une certaine façon, déjà, je traduisais. Quand on parle de mots, n'est-on pas toujours dans l'alchimie d'un processus de traduction ? Rendre l'abstrait — concepts, sentiments, émotions — concret par le biais du langage, voilà tout le projet du langage et, par extension — là où la langue orale doit s'avouer impuissante —, de l'écriture. Pour commencer, s'approprier, puis, partager. Donner forme, pour ainsi dire donner (ou redonner) vie. L'auteur donne et le traducteur redonne.

L'écriture s'est ensuite proposée, très tôt, presque simultanément, comme le moyen privilégié pour arriver à m'exprimer — j'allais dire me libérer. J'inventais des histoires dans ma tête, avec mes poupées, je voulais les «traduire» en mots. (L'auteur serait donc, d'une certaine façon, le premier traducteur de son histoire. Le lecteur en serait un autre, ajoutant sa propre expérience, sa propre compréhension des mots à celles de l'auteur, et ainsi de suite en une chaîne infinie de métamorphoses où chacun, de l'auteur au lecteur, du traducteur au nouveau lecteur, ajoute son grain de sel. Cet « original » après lequel se languissent les puristes serait un leurre, et l'œuvre « achevée », toujours en gestation, puisque toujours en puissance d'être traduite, redonnée à la vie par le traducteur. Ou bien, l'œuvre tradu-ite serait un autre original, susceptible d'être à son tour traduit...)

D'autres rêves, d'autres amours grandirent en même temps. L'amour des sonorités, des mots — ceux de ma propre langue, ceux des langues étrangères. Chaque langue a sa musique. Chaque langue est musique.

that soul, is it untranslatable—impossible to convey? It is also said that poetry is what is inevitably and irredeemably lost in translation. But if the author's poetry is lost, could not the translator's poetry supplant it?)

Translation, treason . . . The two words share a few letters and are easily spoken in one breath. Too easily perhaps. The reason I had trouble believing my ears was that I had never considered translation from such a Manichean point of view. I saw translation more as a generous act, a mission of sorts, designed to spread the good news—good literature. A selfless act, since the sums of money at stake are more often than not derisory given the amount of work involved; and as for glory, there is none.

In my case, it all began with a desire, an urge to speak out. From early childhood, a host of emotions jostled inside me, seeking a way out. From the very first, books kept me company, delighted me. They spoke to me, I identified with the characters; their struggles, their torment became my own. In one way, I was already translating. As for words, are we not always involved in the alchemy of translation? Making what is abstract—concepts, feelings, emotions—concrete through language is the very purpose of language and, by extension, beyond the limits of orality, of writing. Appropriate, then share. Give shape to, give birth (or rebirth) to. The author gives and the translator gives again.

At about the same time, the written word became my preferred method of expression— I almost wrote, of liberation. I made up stories in my head, with my dolls, I wanted to "translate" them into words. (In some way, an author is the first translator of his or her story. The reader is another translator, adding his or her own experience and understanding of the words to the author's, and so on in an infinite chain of metamorphosis where each person, from author to reader, from translator to new reader, adds his or her own grain of salt. The "original" that purists long for is an illusion, while the "completed" work is in constant gestation, since it can always be translated, rebirthed by a translator. Or is it that the translated work becomes another original to be translated in turn . . .?).

Other dreams and loves took hold as well. A love for sound, words—those of my own language and those of foreign languages. Each language has its own music. Each language is music.

J'aurais voulu être musicienne et je n'avais aucun talent. L'écriture fut ma musique. Enfant, j'avais aussi le rêve de jouer, je me voyais sur une scène, cantatrice, comédienne.

Telle que je la perçois, la traduction se rapproche du théâtre. Le traducteur ne joue-t-il pas le rôle de l'auteur qu'il traduit ? Traduire, c'est jouer sans être sur une scène, c'est jouer sans public. Le public vient après, mais on ne le voit jamais, on n'est jamais en sa présence.

Traduire, c'est entrer dans l'autre, trouver sa musique. Trouver les mots en soi pour raconter l'histoire de l'autre. Trouver en soi les émotions qui correspondent à celles de l'autre. Puiser dans sa propre expérience une expérience proche — je ne dis pas «pareille», car rien ne l'est jamais. Se confondre avec l'autre. Se mettre, presque littéralement, «dans la peau de l'autre». Imaginer comment l'autre aurait écrit son histoire s'il l'avait écrite en français — mais l'aurait-il seulement écrite ? Ici, une nouvelle question surgit : l'histoire écrite a-t-elle une langue, a-t-elle besoin d'une langue, ne peut-elle être conçue que dans une seule langue ? Les romans de Dostoïevski ne pouvaient-ils être écrits qu'en russe, *La Recherche du temps perdu*, qu'en français, *Don Quichotte*, qu'en espagnol ? La musique particulière d'une langue est-elle essentielle, pour ainsi dire inhérente au message que l'auteur cherche à communiquer ? Ce message est-il corrompu par son passage dans une autre langue ?

Traduire, c'est interpréter, comme la comédienne interprète Lady Macbeth, le pianiste interprète Bach ou Mozart. Et sait-on comment Bach ou Mozart jouaient leurs pièces ? Comment Shakespeare concevait Ophélie, le roi Lear ? Soupçonne-t-on toujours le metteur en scène ou le comédien de trahir le dramaturge ? Le musicien de trahir le compositeur ? Sans ces interprètes, nous nous retrouverions privés d'émotions capitales, notre expérience de la vie serait bien pauvre. Je ne peux concevoir de ne pas connaître la musique de Bach, mais sans ses interprètes, comment l'aurais-je connue ? Et, au fond, que m'importe de savoir comment il jouait, lui, les *Variations Goldberg* quand Glenn Gould m'en donne sa vision ? Traduire, c'est, en quelque sorte, recréer. Ajouter sa perception, sa sensibilité. Enrichir l'œuvre initiale, voire suppléer parfois, même si cela peut sembler présomptueux de le dire.

L'écriture, ma musique, je l'ai trouvée en moi. L'anglais, je l'ai appris dans la rue, très jeune, ce fut d'abord une langue orale. La langue espagnole je l'ai apprise d'abord à l'école, elle fut d'abord écrite. Plus tard, en Espagne, à l'occasion de nombreux séjours, elle est aussi devenue orale, alors que l'anglais, que je pratique moins, s'est transformé, de par mon travail,

I dreamt of being a musician; I had no talent. The written word was my music. As a child, I dreamt of acting, being on stage, singing professionally. As I see it, translation is like theatre. Doesn't a translator play the role of the author she or he is translating? Translating is acting without a stage, without an audience. The audience comes later, one we never see, never feel.

To translate is to enter into another, find his or her music. Finding the words inside to tell another's story. Finding in oneself the emotions to match the other's. Drawing from one's own experience a similar experience—not "the same" since nothing ever is. To blend with the other. Almost literally, "putting yourself in the skin of the other." Imagining how the other would have written the story were she or he writing in French—but would they have? Another question arises: does a written story have a language, does it need a language, can it be conceived only in one language? Could Dostoyevsky's novels be written only in Russian, *La Recherche du Temps Perdu* only in French, *Don Quijote* only in Spanish? Is the music peculiar to a language essential, actually inherent to the message the author seeks to convey? Is that message corrupted when brought into another language?

To translate is to play a part, like an actress taking on Lady Macbeth, or a pianist taking on Bach or Mozart. Do we know how Bach or Mozart performed their music? How Shakespeare saw Ophelia or King Lear? Are we forever accusing directors or actors of betraying the playwright? Musicians their composer? Without the former, we would be deprived of crucial emotions, and our life experience would be impoverished. I cannot imagine not knowing Bach's music, but without his interpreters, how would I have known it? In actual fact, what do I care how Bach interpreted "The Goldberg Variations" when Glenn Gould gives me his view? To translate, therefore, is in one respect to recreate. Contribute one's perception, sensibility. Enrich the initial work, even supplant it at times, however presumptuous that may sound.

I have found my music—writing—inside me. I learned English on the street at a young age, as an oral language to begin with. I learned Spanish at first in school, as a written language. Later, over the course of many trips to Spain, the language became oral as well while English, which I use less often, became, first and foremost, a written language through my work.

en langue surtout écrite. Et si je les reconnais et comprends leur sens, il m'arrive maintenant de ne plus savoir comment se prononcent les mots anglais que je lis. On pourrait alors se demander comment, dans ce cas, je peux rendre leur musique en français. C'est qu'il existe une musique pour ainsi dire inhérente à la langue écrite, et qu'il n'est pas besoin d'«entendre» les sons pour en sentir la musique. Si, en traduction, la rigueur est indispensable, une large part d'intuition entre aussi en jeu. Ezra Pound affirmait d'ailleurs qu'il n'est pas nécessaire de maîtriser parfaitement une langue pour la traduire — car tout le processus ne se résume pas à une histoire de vases communicants. Rien n'est jamais aussi simple. Heureusement.

La traduction est venue par hasard, mais aussi comme une suite logique. Un jour que j'étais sans travail, un ami m'a proposé un emploi de traductrice. Tel qu'il me présentait la chose, cela semblait aller de soi. Je m'y suis lancée sans réfléchir. J'avais l'impression de réaliser un vieux rêve. J'ai déchanté. Au début, je veux dire.

Comme Éléonore, la traductrice que j'ai créée dans mes romans, j'ai commencé par ce que j'appelle la Manufacture de Mots, c'est-à-dire un bureau de traduction, une dure école, une expérience éprouvante. Très loin du théâtre, de la musique. Très loin de la création. Et pourtant, tout texte écrit, même le plus banal, le plus redondant, le plus pompeux, le plus vide, tout texte écrit ne mérite-t-il pas de l'être bien ? N'a-t-il pas aussi sa musique — même monotone ? Le musicien qui apprend à jouer ne commence-t-il pas par des gammes ? Mais alors, peut-on dire que répéter inlassablement do ré mi fa sol sur un clavier, c'est jouer du piano, que vocaliser, c'est chanter ? Moi, j'ai déchanté parce que j'avais placé la barre trop haut. Partie pour ma croisade, je me voyais parcourir, éblouie, les paysages fabuleux du langage. C'est dire combien je fus prise de vertige, de nausée parfois, devant l'aridité des textes que j'avais à traduire, une prose souvent boiteuse, enchevêtrée, maladroite, obscure, truffée de termes techniques inconnus, de concepts confus, une prose qu'il me fallait pourtant comprendre et rendre dans un français clair et précis.

Écriture et traduction se sont bientôt mêlées. C'est à la Manufacture de Mots que le personnage d'Éléonore a vu le jour. Je gardais un cahier à côté de moi, dans lequel j'écrivais sur elle entre deux descriptions de poste, deux procès-verbaux de réunion de comité. Elle fut tout de suite mon double. Je traduisais en rêvant, et j'écrivais sur elle qui rêvait en traduisant. Je lui faisais traduire ce que je traduisais — et la journée était moins longue. Je lui donnais mes rêves et mes terreurs. J'en inventais pour elle. Elle est

Although I recognize and understand the meaning of words in English, sometimes I now no longer know how to pronounce the words I read. One might wonder then how I am able to convey their music in French. It is because there is a music inherent to the written language; sounds do not need to be "heard" for their music to be felt. Although rigour is a must in translation, intuition also has an important role to play. Ezra Pound stated that one does not need a perfect command of a language to translate it—since the process cannot be boiled down to one of communicating vessels. Nothing is ever that simple. Fortunately.

I came to translate by chance, but also as a logical consequence. One day I found myself unemployed and a friend offered me a job as a translator. He made it seem like a natural choice. I jumped at the opportunity without a second thought. It felt as if I was making an old dream come true. I soon became disenchanted. At first, I mean.

Like Éléonore, the translator I created in my novels, I began in what I call the Word Factory, that is, a translation office, a tough school, a trying time. Far from theatre and music. Far from creation. Yet doesn't every written text no matter how banal, how redundant, how pompous, how empty, deserve to be well done? Don't they all also have their own music—monotonous as it may be? Don't musicians learning to play begin with scales? Then again, can it be said that endlessly repeating do-re-mi-fa-sol on a piano keyboard is equivalent to playing the piano, or that vocalizing is singing? I became disenchanted because I put the bar too high. At the start of my crusade, I saw myself, dazzled, attaining the fabulous landscapes of language. What vertigo, what nausea at times, at the dryness of the texts I had to translate, often lame, convoluted, awkward, obscure prose riddled with unknown technical terms, confusing concepts, prose I nevertheless had to understand and render in clear, precise French.

The practice of writing and translation soon merged. My character Éléonore first saw the light of day in the Word Factory. I kept a notebook by my side in which I wrote about her between two job descriptions, two sets of committee minutes. She was my double from the start. I translated as if in a dream and wrote about her dreaming as she translated. I had her translate what I was translating—making my day seem not quite as long. I gave her my dreams and fears and invented them for her. She was born

née d'un fantasme, elle est née dans un fantasme, dans la nouvelle «Les fantasmes d'Éléonore», la première nouvelle que j'ai écrite.

Le recueil qui a suivi s'appelle *L'homme de Hong Kong*. «Les fantasmes» l'ouvrent, «L'homme de Hong Kong», la nouvelle éponyme, le clôt. L'homme de Hong Kong est un assassin en fuite, il n'a pas encore de nom. Pour le créer, je me suis inspirée d'un fait divers : un tueur en série dont j'avais entendu parler à la radio, qui torturait ses victimes, filmait leur agonie et vendait les cassettes. Mort en direct, destinée aux amateurs de sensations très fortes. Bien sûr, il y a vingt-cinq ans, on parlait peu de ces choses — elles ne faisaient pas encore partie de notre quotidien — et j'avais eu un choc. À la fin de la nouvelle, une femme passe devant le tueur, et j'ai eu l'intuition que c'était Éléonore, qu'une rencontre déterminante devait avoir lieu entre les deux protagonistes.

Puis, j'ai écrit *Les miroirs d'Éléonore* où elle est peintre — une autre façon, si l'on veut, de traduire la réalité. C'est-à-dire qu'elle occupe encore une position d'intermédiaire entre la réalité et sa représentation. Dans ce roman, le tueur a maintenant un nom, il rôde à la périphérie de chacun des chapitres, présence menaçante, lourde, infiniment inquiétante. La rencontre n'a pas lieu, mais elle est latente, imminente. Elle s'impose. Je ne savais pas encore comment la mettre en scène.

Dans *Chambre avec baignoire*, Éléonore est de nouveau traductrice, elle rêve d'écrire, mais l'écriture est hors de portée. La traduction est un pis-aller, elle la pratique sans y croire, la regarde de haut, la tourne — se tourne — en dérision. Elle a quitté la Manufacture de Mots pour passer à la traduction de romans d'amour, la collection «Sentiments».

Déjà, dans mon inconscient — puisque dans la conscience de mon personnage —, se posait la question de la responsabilité. Dans quelle mesure le traducteur est-il responsable de ce qu'il traduit ? Où commence et où s'achève son engagement ? Et quand je parle de responsabilité, d'engagement, je ne parle pas seulement de la responsabilité du traducteur par rapport au fond et à la forme — au sens et au style — du texte qu'on lui confie. Bien que ce soit là la responsabilité première du traducteur, ce serait trop simple, réducteur. Ainsi, il m'est arrivé de traduire des rapports, des comptes rendus que je savais truffés de demi-mensonges, de la publicité que je savais frauduleuse. Étais-je responsable ? À qui devais-je être fidèle, à moi-même ou à la personne que je traduisais ? La personne que je traduisais me faisais confiance, avais-je le droit de la tromper ? Mais, en traduisant ses mensonges, en en étant consciente, ne me trahissais-je pas moi-même ?

of the dreamworld, born in the dreamworlds in the story "Les fantasmes d'Éléonore," the first short story I wrote.

The collection that ensued was entitled *L'homme de Hong Kong*. It opens with "Les fantasmes d'Éléonore" and "L'homme de Hong Kong," the eponymous short story, brings it to a close. The man from Hong Kong is a killer on the run, as yet without a name. To create him, I sought inspiration in a news item: a serial killer I heard about on the radio who tortured his victims, filmed their dying moments and sold the tapes. Death shown live, as it were, aimed at thrill-seekers. Of course, twenty-five years ago, such stories were rarely mentioned in the news—they were not yet part of our daily fare—and I was shocked. At the end of the short story, a woman crosses the killer's path and intuitively I knew that the woman was Éléonore, and that a decisive encounter must take place between the two protagonists.

Then I wrote *Les miroirs d'Éléonore* in which she is an artist, another way if you will of translating reality. In other words, she occupies yet another intermediary position between reality and its representation. In the novel, the killer now has a name, he haunts the periphery of every chapter, a threatening, portentous, infinitely disturbing presence. The encounter never takes place, yet all the while it is latent, imminent. Inescapable. I still had no idea how to set it up.

In *Room with Bath*, Éléonore is a translator again dreaming of writing, but that is beyond her reach. Translation is a compromise, a profession she practises without conviction, looks down on, speaks of—both it and her-self—derisively. She has left the Word Factory to begin translating romance novels in the "Sentiments" collection.

Given that it was in the conscious mind of my character, the issue of responsibility must have already arisen in my unconscious. To what extent is a translator responsible for what she translates? Where does her commit-ment begin and end? When I refer to responsibility and commitment, I do not just mean a translator's responsibility to the content and form—mean-ing and style—of a text entrusted to her. The translator's first responsibility may be that, but it cannot be reduced to that. I have translated reports and minutes riddled with half-truths and advertising I knew to be false. Did that make me responsible? To whom must I be faithful, myself or the person I translated? Those writers trusted me, did I have a right to deceive them? But by translating what I knew to be lies, was I not betraying myself?

Je n'ai pas fait comme Éléonore, mais j'ai entrepris la traduction littéraire par une série de romans de Lucy Maud Montgomery, qui m'ont plongée dans un univers à l'opposé de mes préoccupations. Un nouvel élément se greffait pourtant à mon travail : l'aspect ludique, le plaisir, cette recherche de la musique de l'autre dont je parlais tout à l'heure. Et j'ai ainsi eu la possibilité de pratiquer certaines techniques que je maîtrisais mal dans ma propre écriture, l'humour et l'art du dialogue, par exemple. De cette façon, la pratique de la traduction a enrichi mon écriture — l'œuvre à traduire nourrissait en moi l'écrivain malhabile. Chacun des livres que j'ai traduits m'a appris quelque chose. Prendre et donner.

C'est cette expérience qui m'a donné l'idée de faire d'Éléonore une traductrice de romans d'amour. Bien sûr, ce n'était pas mon cas et, malgré toute sa candeur, Anne d'Avonlea n'est pas une héroïne de romans Harlequin. Mais il y a dans l'œuvre de Lucy Maud Montgomery un côté profondément optimiste très loin de moi.

Je n'oubliais pas le tueur et sa confrontation avec Éléonore. Dans *Chambre avec baignoire*, Éléonore parle d'un enfant, sa fille morte à trois ans dans des circonstances mystérieuses. J'ai alors voulu imaginer ce que ce pourrait être pour elle — par ricochet, pour moi aussi, sans doute —, que de traduire l'autobiographie du tueur. J'ai voulu la faire réfléchir — et j'ai voulu réfléchir en même temps — aux choix éthiques que peut parfois poser la traduction. Que peut-on accepter de traduire ? Jusqu'à quel point s'engage-t-on dans une traduction ? Comment une femme qui a elle-même perdu un enfant peut-elle traduire l'histoire d'un homme qui assassine les enfants ? J'ai délibérément choisi une situation extrême.

Il ne pouvait exister de rapport plus intime. Entrer dans l'autre, se confondre, dans le meilleur des cas, avec l'autre, l'espace d'un moment privilégié. J'avais d'abord pensé à une rencontre de type charnel entre le tueur et la traductrice, puis, j'ai compris que cela ne suffirait pas. En traduisant l'autobiographie du tueur, Éléonore s'engage : elle veut comprendre, le comprendre. Elle endosse le « je » d'un personnage qu'elle exècre, avec ce « je », elle décrit les actes terribles qu'il a faits, avec ce «je», elle va jusqu'à torturer — virtuellement — un enfant.

En faisant cette traduction, Éléonore se met aussi en danger. Délibérément. « J'écoute la voix exécrable de Leonard Ming et celle de la mer. Je voudrais traduire comme si de rien n'était, comme si ce n'était qu'un travail banal, aligner des mots sans me préoccuper de leur charge émotive. Non pas traductrice de sentiments, mais de mots, comme une machine», pense-t-elle parfois. C'est impossible. « Je pourrais arrêter de traduire ce

I did not follow in Éléonore's footsteps. I began translating literature through Lucy Maud Montgomery's novels, finding myself in a universe quite the opposite of my own concerns. Yet a new element was grafted onto my work: playfulness, pleasure, that quest for another's music I just mentioned. I was thus given an opportunity to employ certain techniques I had little command of in my own writing—humour and dialogue, for instance. Hence the practice of translation enriched my own writing—the novel being translated fed my inner writer lacking in skill. Each book I translated taught me something. A process of give and take.

The experience gave me the idea of making Éléonore become a translator of romance novels. Not what I was doing, of course, and despite all her naïveté, Anne of Avonlea is far from a Harlequin heroine. But Lucy Maud Montgomery's work has a profoundly optimistic bent to it that is very foreign to me.

I had not forgotten about the killer and his confrontation with Éléonore. In *Room with Bath*, Éléonore speaks of a child, her daughter who died at the age of three under mysterious circumstances. I wanted to imagine what it would be like for her—for me, too, indirectly no doubt—to translate a killer's autobiography. I wanted her to ponder—at the same time I did—the ethical choices that can sometimes crop up with a translation. What should one agree to translate? How committed must one be to a translation? How can a woman who has lost a child herself translate the story of a man who kills children? I deliberately chose an extreme situation.

There could be no closer relationship. To penetrate another, become one, in the best-case scenario, with another, for a privileged moment. At first, I imagined a carnal encounter between the killer and the translator, then I understood that would not be enough. In translating the killer's autobiography, Éléonore has made a choice: she wants to understand, understand him. She shoulders the "I" of a person she abhors; with the "I" she describes his horrendous acts; with the "I" she goes so far as to torture—virtually—a child.

Through the translation, Éléonore also puts herself in danger's way. Deliberately. "I listen to the execrable voice of Leonard Ming and that of the sea. I would like to translate as if it were nothing, only a mundane job, stringing words on a page without worrying about their emotional power. Not a translator of love, but of words, like a machine," she sometimes thinks. An impossibility. "I could stop translating this book, stop being

livre, sortir de l'engrenage. Ne plus traduire que de la poésie que personne ne lirait, mais qu'importe puisque, en la traduisant, je lui donnerais vie à nouveau ? Ajouter à la beauté du monde plutôt qu'à sa laideur. »

C'est, bien sûr, une tentation. La beauté. La beauté initiale d'un texte serait le moteur de la traduction. Il y a certes quelque chose de profondément séduisant dans cette façon de voir la traduction. Je dois pourtant admettre que j'ai traduit des textes que je ne trouvais pas nécessairement « beaux » d'entrée de jeu. Je veux dire que, parfois, leur écriture ne correspondait pas à mon esthétique. Des livres que je trouvais même rébarbatifs, peuplés de personnages à des années-lumière des miens, pratiquant des métiers, des activités dont je n'avais aucune idée. L'effort exigé est énorme. C'est ainsi que je me suis retrouvée dans des histoires de pêche à la morue à Terre-Neuve, ou au milieu de faussaires, à Londres, à l'époque du roi George III, ou encore en compagnie de chevaliers en armure dans une France médiévale mythique. Le défi qui se pose alors en est d'autant plus grand. Je dois faire totalement abstraction de moi, m'absenter de moi-même, adhérer à une musique, à une esthétique, à des émotions qui me sont étrangères. Utiliser des mots, des temps de verbe, une syntaxe qui n'auraient pas leur place dans mes propres livres... « Seule avec l'acte d'écrire », pour reprendre l'expression du traducteur/écrivain Louis Jolicœur. Seule avec une histoire que je n'aurais jamais pu moi-même écrire. D'une certaine façon, je dirais que moins un livre me ressemble, plus j'éprouve de plaisir à le traduire. Réflexe de comédienne frustrée à la recherche de rôles de composition ?

L'expérience peut-être la plus troublante que j'ai vécue en traduction a été quand j'ai traduit *Self*, de Yann Martel. Dans ce roman, le personnage, d'abord masculin, se transforme, au fil de l'histoire, en fille. Le défi consistait à rendre ce « je » féminin non pas comme moi, femme, l'aurait écrit, mais comme l'avait écrit un homme essayant de comprendre « de l'intérieur » ce qu'est une femme. De rendre donc ce « je » avec le décalage que je percevais. Me transformer en homme se transformant en femme.

J'ai dit plus tôt qu'il y a une vingtaine d'années, on parlait moins de tueurs en série et de mort en direct. Ces choses existaient-elles moins parce qu'on en parlait moins ? La multitude de livres, de films, de reportages sur le sujet qui ont déferlé sur le marché a-t-elle un effet d'entraînement ? En réalité, je n'en sais rien, mais je crois que, prenant conscience de cela, le traducteur fait un choix éthique lorsqu'il accepte de traduire ce genre de livre. Refuser de traduire une œuvre qui heurte ses convictions profondes

dragged down by it. Only translate poetry that no one will read, but what's the difference, because by translating it I'll be bringing it to life again? Adding to the beauty of the world rather than to its ugliness." (*Reading Nijinski,* tr. by Jonathan Kaplansky, XYZ Publishing, 2001)

So tempting. Beauty. The initial beauty of a text as the driving force for translation. There is something profoundly seductive about such a perspective on translation. Yet I have to admit I have translated texts I did not necessarily find "beautiful" to begin with. Some because the style did not meet my aesthetic criteria. Other books I found daunting even, peopled with characters light years from my own experience, practicing professions and activities I knew nothing about. The effort required is enormous. It brought me to cod fishing stories in Newfoundland or among counterfeiters in the London of George III, or in the midst of armoured knights in a mythical medieval France. The challenge there is even greater. I have to step outside myself, leave myself behind, follow a music, aesthetics, and emotions that are foreign to me. Use words, verb tenses and a syntax that would be jarring in my own books . . . "Alone with the act of writing," to quote translator/writer Louis Jolicoeur. Alone with a story I could never have written myself. In one way, I could say that the less a book resembles me, the more pleasure I take in translating it. Could it be the reflex of a frustrated actor seeking parts to sink her teeth into?

Perhaps the most troubling translation experience I have ever had was translating Yann Martel's *Self.* In that novel, the character, male to begin with, transforms into a female over the course of the story. The challenge was to make the female "I" something other than what I, a woman, would have written, but what a man would write trying to understand a woman "from inside." To render the "I" with the dissonance I perceived. Make of myself a man become a woman.

I mentioned earlier that twenty years ago there was less talk of serial killers and death "live." Did these things exist any the less because they were less talked about? Have the many books, movies, documentaries that have flooded the market on the subject had a snowball effect? I have no idea, in truth, but I do believe that, being aware of the possibility, the translator makes an ethical choice when agreeing to translate such a book. Refusing to translate a book that clashes with a translator's deepest beliefs would

placerait cette fois le traducteur devant le problème de la censure, un autre choix relevant de l'éthique. Les œuvres morales, celles qui correspondent à notre conception du bien sont-elles les seules dignes d'être traduites ? À ce compte-là, aucun comédien n'accepterait de jouer le rôle d'Iago, et sans Iago, la tragédie d'*Othello* n'aurait pas lieu.

Je n'ai, pour ma part, jamais eu à faire ce genre de choix. Après Lucy Maud Montgomery, j'ai traduit les nouvelles, les romans et les essais d'auteurs comme Yann Martel, Julie Keith, Bernice Morgan, Taras Grescoe, Gustavo Sainz, Jeffrey Moore, Wayson Choy, Madeleine Thien. Chaque fois, j'entre en eux, en traduisant leurs histoires, je m'approche de leur vérité, je joue leur musique sur mon instrument. Je m'approche aussi de la mienne, car la traduction est un miroir. Dans ce miroir se reflètent toutes les facettes de mon être, l'inavouable autant que l'avouable, l'histoire vécue comme l'histoire rêvée.

mean censorship, another choice based on ethics. Are moral works, those that fit our view of good, the only ones worthy of being translated? In that case, no actor would ever agree to play the role of Iago, and without Iago, the tragedy of *Othello* would not exist.

I myself have never had to make that kind of choice. After Lucy Maud Montgomery, I translated short stories, novels and non-fiction by authors such as Yann Martel, Julie Keith, Bernice Morgan, Taras Grescoe, Gustavo Sainz, Jeffrey Moore, Wayson Choy, Madeleine Thien. Every time I enter into them, translating their stories, drawing nearer to their truth, I play their music on my instrument. I also draw nearer to my own truth, since translation is a mirror. That mirror reflects all the facets of my being, what can and cannot be confessed, life as it is lived and life as it is dreamt.

Translation by S. Ouriou

Translating Fictions:
The Messenger was a Medium

Lazer Lederhendler

The American translator Eliot Weinberger has remarked
that "one can never mention the word "translation" without some wit
bringing up—as though for the first time—that tedious Italian pun
traduttore traditore" (5). Weinberger dismantles the "translator = traitor"
equation by demonstrating that the "Utopian dream of exact equivalences"
upheld largely by "members of foreign language departments"—whom he
portrays as the shock troops of the "translation police" (6)—is a specious
standard for measuring a translation's worth. He argues that a translation
is essentially a reading, and no reading, whether within or across languages, can or should be identical to the original text or to any other reading of
that text. It is probably no accident that this approach should be consistent
with the one articulated by Octavio Paz, whose poetry has been made available to English readers thanks mainly to Eliot Weinberger's translations.
Paz writes, "No text can be completely original because language itself, in
its very essence, is already a translation— first from the non-verbal world,
and then, because each sign and each phrase is a translation of another
sign, another phrase" (154). Thus, "reading is translation within the same
language" (159). In sum, both Paz and Weinberger refute the charge of
treason brought against the translator on the grounds that translation, and
so by extension the translator, is a medium and as such must unavoidably
transform the mediated work if it is to come alive in another language.
And without the translator's mediation, Weinberger furthermore
concludes, literature cannot live.

Adopting a somewhat different approach, the structuralist linguist Roman
Jakobson, in his essay "On Linguistic Aspects of Translation," interrogates
the *traduttore traditore* formula in specifically socio-linguistic terms:
"[A] cognitive attitude would compel us to change this aphorism into a
more explicit statement and to answer the questions: translator of what
messages? betrayer of what values?" (435). For Jakobson, then, the two-
faced nature of the translator—at once messenger and medium/betray-
er— is a given. And the way those two faces are framed can justifiably be
viewed in terms of the historical, cultural, ethical—in a word, political—
functions of translation.

Thus, by virtue of the intrinsic operations of her work, the translator is at least to some degree involved in an intrigue where version must perforce engender a subversion of the original. In the early history of translation this drama of version and subversion emerges most famously in the activity of Saint Jerome, patron of translators. As Lawrence Venuti explains in *The Scandals of Translation,* "Augustine, bishop of Hippo, feared Jerome's project of translating the Old Testament directly from the Hebrew because it threatened the ideological consistency and institutional stability of the Church" (78).

Much later, in the new world, translation had lost none of its political impact. When the first Europeans arrived in what would come to be known as the Americas, translation among the various indigenous peoples had been a well-established fact of social life for thousands of years. According to anthropologist Harold E. Driver, "There were bilingual and even trilingual persons within each social group who could translate when the occasion required" (25). However, the earliest documented cases of translational subversion occurred after the arrival of the European colonial powers. Specifically, in 1535, Jacques Cartier committed a consequential error of over-translation when he referred to all the lands under the sway of Donnacona, chief of Stadacona, as *Canada,* a French rendering of *kanata,* the Huron-Iroquoian term for "village" or "settlement," which Cartier first learned from Donnacona's sons Domagaya and Taignoagy (Lamb). Translation scholars Pamela Grant and Kathy Mezei, drawing on the work of Jean Delisle, furthermore point out that Cartier, through "a violent and coercive act," had taken these two young men back to France in 1534 so that they might later serve as interpreters when he returned to New France. "Thus," Grant and Mezei write, "from early on, translation [in Canada] has borne the stigma of cultural appropriation and colonial exploitation. With both French and English being given official status by the language provisions of the BNA Act of 1867 and by the federal Official Languages Act of 1969, translation has been rooted in political contingency."

This assessment corroborates an earlier appraisal by Pierre Cardinal, who explains that consequent to the rise of French Canadian nationalism in the 1940s and 50s and to the impact of the Quiet Revolution in Quebec in the 1960s, the official "bilingualisation" of Canada became a necessity, and translation a "politically indispensable" activity (142). Writing in 1977, Cardinal shows that the overwhelming balance of (pragmatic) translations at the time were from English to French, due to the dominant position of

Anglophones in both government and business. On one level there is, as Cardinal demonstrates, the need for the largely English-speaking Federal administration not only to communicate its policies to the French-speaking minority but also to make that minority feel included in "the life of the country." At the same time, private enterprises run by Anglophones find themselves under rising pressure to translate their publicity into French to increase sales and, more generally, to enhance their corporate image among the French-speaking public. Cardinal concludes that "[t]ranslation has become a buffer institution between our two national groups... The institution of translation thus plays an eminently political—though apparently modest—role in Canadian society... These circumstances cast doubt, at least for the time being, on much of the supposed benefits of translation for the maintenance of our cultural identity and of our rights to equal opportunity" (146). So translation is here identified as a means to subvert, even to betray, the democratic national aspirations of the Québécois. If one strictly follows this line of thinking, government and business translators in the 70s—a majority of whom, Cardinal notes, were French-speaking — could be considered "traitors" vis-à-vis their community. In fact, however, the situation is rather more complex, because among other things the increased availability of government documents in French has represented a recognition of Francophone rights and a concession to the social and political clout that French-speaking Canadians (not only in Quebec) achieved after years of protesting and lobbying in various arenas.

But what of literary translation? According to Grant and Mezei, "In the 1960s and 70s, in the face of Quebec's deep discontent and fears about its cultural and linguistic survival, literary translation, especially from French to English, began to flourish." So, while most pragmatic translations during this period were from English into French, most literary translations were in the opposite direction. Various sociological explanations have been proposed to account for this apparent paradox, such as the far lower rate of bilingualism among the English-speaking readers, or the desire among Francophone publishers to focus their efforts on affirming and fostering French, particularly French Canadian, literature, rather than translations of English writing, faced with the monopolistic tendencies of English. Whatever their merits, however, such hypotheses are by and large premised on a viewpoint outside the lived experience of translators themselves, especially those working from French to English, during those crucial years. What motivated them? And, to return to Jakobson's line of questioning, what messages were they translating? What values were they betraying?

Bearing News from Abroad: 1970 and Beyond

I think it would be appropriate at this point to adopt an autobiographical approach to such questions. Within the whole momentous period of the Sixties and Seventies, there are good reasons to flag 1970 as a watershed year. For one thing, it was in 1970 that the pre-eminent English translator of Québécois fiction, Sheila Fischman, published her first translation: Roch Carrier's *La Guerre, Yes Sir!* It was also the year of the first public reading of Michèle Lalonde's now classic poetic denunciation of linguistic colonialism, "Speak White." But 1970 was above all the year of the October Crisis and P.E. Trudeau's invocation of the War Measures Act. This also turned out to be the year when I undertook my first serious attempt at translating a French text into English. The source text begins as follows: *"Le Front de libération du Québec n'est pas le messie, ni un Robin des bois des temps modernes. C'est un regroupement de travailleurs québécois qui sont décidés à tout mettre en œuvre pour que le peuple du Québec prenne définitivement en mains son destin."* This, of course, was the FLQ Manifesto. At the time, I was sharing a large flat with six or seven people half of whom were Francophone Québécois, and the other half a variety of English-speakers including another born and bred Montrealer like myself. The flat was located in what is now the trendy Plateau Mont-Royal district but which in those days was viewed by most local Anglophones as simply the East, east, that is, of Boulevard Saint-Laurent, the historical boundary between English and French Montreal. My migration from one to the other—which I long regarded as a process of changing countries without changing cities—was in many ways similar to the one mapped out by Sherry Simon in *Translating Montreal: Episodes in the Life of a Divided City.* In my case, the intellectual baggage that I carried eastward was of the far-left variety. Hence it was not particularly difficult for me to shift from a strong identification with Meursault, the alienated protagonist of Albert Camus' *L'Étranger* (that I had discovered as a very young undergraduate in a French literature course at McGill University, that bastion of Anglo-bourgeois power) to a passionate identification with the intrepid narrator of Pierre Vallière's *Les nègres blancs d'Amérique* (my first extracurricular encounter with a book-length French narrative, which I read upon landing in the East). This takes on relevance to the extent that among the elements that compelled me to begin translating the Manifesto within hours of its publication [said broadcast and publication being one of the conditions set by the FLQ for the release of their hostage, British Trade Commissioner Richard Cross] was its decidedly pro-working-class, anti-capitalist outlook, conveyed through its radical

political and economic analysis as well as its brutally iconoclastic language peppered with *joual*. Indeed, for many of us witnessing the events, the very fact such things were being said and printed in the mainstream media was in itself a revolutionary occurrence on a par with, perhaps to some extent overshadowing, the Manifesto's contents. And likewise, it seemed to me, its translation into English. As a fledgling translator feverishly cutting his teeth on an important, albeit not quite literary, text I was naturally stimulated by both its subject matter and its translational challenges. But I was at least equally excited by the mere idea of smuggling the forbidden text—which through my intervention had now been made to "speak white" —back across the French-English dividing-line. (I was soon to discover that I was far from alone. After dashing off the translation I hurried over to a hush-hush meeting at McGill University that had been hastily convened by a Marxist-Feminist sociologist who had migrated north from the USA. I proudly deposited my translation on the professor's desk and saw half a dozen other English versions of the FLQ Manifesto already laid out there. As an epilogue to this anecdote I recently learned from a fellow translator that he had had much the same experience at the same time in Toronto.)

Thus, when I entered the history of translation in Canada I was clearly acting as a messenger or, as Weinberger puts it, bearer of "genuine news from abroad" (2), however nearby "abroad" may be. The message, however, cannot be reduced simply to the Manifesto's statement. For, just as the transmission of the FLQ's message via the capitalist-controlled media made visible not just this or that particular power relationship but the very mechanism of mediation, so too the very act of translating that statement into English betrayed not only the status of the English language as a colonial instrument but also shed light on language itself as a medium acting upon our perception of reality. More recently, more than 35 years after the October Crisis, I had the privilege of translating Nicolas Dickner's novel *Nikolski*. The position of *Nikolski* as a milestone in the literary landscape of Quebec has been confirmed by its inclusion in *Histoire de la littérature québécoise* (published in August 2007), the first major historical survey of Québécois literature to appear in forty years and whose chronology begins with Jacques Cartier's travelogue (alluded to above) and actually closes with *Nikolski* (Fr 631, Eng 649). The primary justification for this, in my view, is that this mischievous, multi-layered narrative, composed with the diabolical, mathematical precision of an Escher engraving, frames a new, ground-breaking vision not just of but *from* Quebec. And, with reference to Roman Jakobson's first question— "translator of what message?"—

to relay the scope, detail, and colour of the vision enacted in and by the text was and is the challenge facing us as translators.

By way of circumscribing that vision it may be helpful at the outset to explain that *Nikolski* traces the intersecting trajectories of three people who, unbeknownst to any of them, have blood ties thanks to Jonas Doucet, a seafarer born in Tête-à-la-Baleine, Quebec, and buried in Nikolski, a hamlet in the Aleutian Islands. Two of the protagonists are Jonas's offspring by different mothers. The first, an unnamed clerk in a Borgesian second-hand bookstore in Montreal, never knew his father and has only a toy compass forever pointing toward Nikolski to remember him by. The second, Noah Riel, learned to read by studying roadmaps while crisscrossing the Prairies in an old station wagon driven by his Chipewyan mother Sarah. Noah goes off to study archaeology at the Université du Québec à Montréal (UQAM) and eventually lands on Margarita Island, Venezuela. The third protagonist is Joyce Doucet, Jonas's niece and descendant of a long line of Acadian pirates. Joyce runs away from Quebec's Lower North Shore to Montreal, where, following in the footsteps of her mother, who vanished just after Joyce's birth, she embarks on a career of computer piracy.

Thus, central to the vision represented in Nikolski are on the one hand the construction and constructedness of identity and genealogy and heritage on the other. Mobile individual space-time coordinates on the one hand and, on the other, interconnectedness, both visible and secret. Furthermore, while the vision is hemispheric and planetary in extent, it moves along the axis of a constantly shifting perspective that zooms into and out from a local, personal position: Canada, Quebec, Montreal, Little Italy, an apartment, a room, a bed, a thought. This mechanism is set in motion already in the opening episode, where the narrator, still half-asleep, is convinced that he is hearing waves breaking on a shore somewhere on Earth and struggles to identify the exact location, only to realize that the sound is coming from a garbage truck in suburban Montreal. The global therefore does not, must not, obviate the specific in Nikolski. The translator (not to mention the publisher) needs to resist the globalizing temptation of allowing Montreal's *Petite Italie* to become indistinguishable from the Little Italies of Toronto, Boston, or Manchester, for to do so would effect a grave distortion of the organic view of the relationship between the planetary and the particular developed in the novel. Another, more microscopic, case in point: In one scene, the clerk at the loans counter of the

UQAM library is reading Gabrielle Roy's *La Route d'Altamont* (Fr 142, Eng 124). Now, a perfectly good English translation—by Joyce Marshall—of Roy's novel exists under the title *The Road Past Altamont*. But to have substituted one for the other here would have severely obscured the specificity of the setting: library clerks in the Université du Québec à Montréal do not as a rule read English translations of French-Canadian authors.

It becomes obvious at this point that Jakobson's two questions cannot be answered separately. As evidenced in *Nikolski*, the vision produced through the narrative gives form to a body of values that at the same time inform that vision. Consequently, to distort the vision inevitably entails a skewing of those values. The potential for such misrepresentations are often found lurking in the tiny folds of a novel's body politic. For instance, the expression "*l'An de grâce*" (230), which one would quite naturally be inclined to render in English as "year of our Lord." In the context of Nikolski, however, eschewing the less usual, more dated "year of grace" (206) would implicate the translator in a seemingly minor but in fact egregious violation of both the vision and the values that this novel stages. First, because the Christian allusion would be incongruent with the marked absence in the text of religious references. Second, because this absence bespeaks (in a sense betrays) the secularity that is a crucial legacy of the Quiet Revolution and a hallmark of contemporary Quebec, as well as an essential element of the conceptual environment where *Nikolski*'s characters and narrators live and breathe. Certain translational betrayals, however, are much harder to avoid, as they seem to arise out of the very DNA of prose fiction. In the concluding moments of *Nikolski*, Noah is in Montreal trying to make a collect call to Venezuela. An international operator answers:

> **"Hi-bonsoir-comment-puis-je-vous-aider-how-can-I-help-you?"**
> **For a few seconds Noah is thrown off balance. The accent seems to be neither Québécois nor American nor Latin American, but a sort of amalgam originating in every place and no place at the same time, as if the voice did not really belong to a human being but to a spurt of DNA designed to meet a specific need and then injected into the circuits of the telephone system. An entity with no accent, no nationality and no trade-union demands (Fr 307-308, Eng 274).**

This passage brings into stark relief one of the areas where the translator is most vulnerable to treason: dialogue. Fictional narrative's overall effect vitally depends on characterization, whose success in turn depends so much on the convincing performance of dialogue, yet the translator is generally expected to make the characters express themselves with native

fluency in a language which is not their own. As a result, the Québécois and French-Canadian characters in *Nikolski* are in danger of being not just left with "no accent, no nationality" but effectively absorbed into the vast international waters of English. This may be one area where the "foreignizing" strategy, proposed most notably by Lawrence Venuti, may open up interesting alternative avenues and prospects.

All this points to the conclusion that whatever devices translators may deploy, we cannot ultimately outmanoeuvre the intrinsic operations of translation as a medium. We may enjoy some freedom in choosing to transport this or that message across the language barrier because of its political import or power to subvert, the fact remains, to quote Robert Eaglestone's paraphrasing of Paul de Man, that "what I translate is upset by the way I translate" (137) because "[W]hat I mean is upset by the way I mean" (135). What the translator betrays, then, has much to do with the "politics" of the translated message and the political, geo-political stakes of the act of translation, but ultimately she also betrays her own status and the status of translation as medium, and by inference the unmentionable fact that all human experience is "always already" mediated, language being the primal, primary medium. One is reminded of Jim Carrey in Peter Weir's film *The Truman Show*, literally poking his finger through the envelope of "reality." This, fundamentally, is why in the publishing world translations are required to be utterly legible yet perfectly transparent, why translators may be read but never seen, much less heard. Their visibility would be a huge embarrassment, a shocking betrayal.

Les humanistes

Nicolas Dickner

Le campus du Banff Centre est éparpillé à flanc de colline, à travers des pins et des épinettes, à l'ombre de cette impossibilité géologique que l'on nomme le mont Rundle.

Des douzaines d'artistes de toutes les disciplines se côtoient dans cet endroit qui tient à la fois du monastère, du complexe scientifique et de la réserve faunique. Cette petite communauté carbure essentiellement au café : on en concocte (et consomme) des kilolitres depuis l'aube jusqu'au crépuscule. Après quelques jours au centre, plus personne ne dort : la veine temporale palpite et bat le rythme jusqu'aux petites heures.

C'est dans cet endroit singulier que le Banff International Literary Translation Centre m'a invité à passer la semaine, en compagnie d'une vingtaine de traducteurs d'un peu partout dans le monde.

Instructif séjour, en vérité. Depuis mon arrivée, les échanges quotidiens se déroulent en anglais, français et espagnol, avec des accents latino-américains et anglo-saxons, bulgares, coréens, cris, québécois et norvégiens — ce qui engendre à tout moment un chaos proprement babélien.

Et de quoi discutent les traducteurs en résidence? De lexicologie, de ponctuation, de prosodie polonaise et de métrique castillane, de *Don Quichotte* et de William Faulkner, et encore de William Faulkner, de sémantique et d'intention, d'onomastique galicienne, de ton, de style, de philologie, des étonnants défis documentaires que pose *Moby Dick* — et, accessoirement, du plat du jour à la cafétéria.

Même en plein *small talk*, ils s'arrêtent périodiquement afin d'analyser la façon dont se déroule la discussion. Le cerveau du traducteur n'arrête jamais de travailler puisque tout, dans l'univers, est matière à traduction — depuis les gesticulations de l'interlocuteur jusqu'au goutte à goutte du robinet de la cuisine, en passant par le parcours des nuages sur le flanc de la montagne et les couinements des spermophiles (ces rongeurs paranoïaques qui infestent le campus).

The Humanists

Nicolas Dickner

Dotted along a hillside amongst spruce and pine trees in the shadow of the geological impossibility called Rundle Mountain is The Banff Centre campus.

Dozens of artists from all disciplines rub shoulders in this place, which is something of a monastery, scientific complex and nature reserve all rolled into one. The small community runs primarily on coffee; kilolitres are prepared (and consumed) from dawn to dusk. After a few days in the centre, people quit sleeping; their temporal vein palpitates and beats time until the wee hours of the morning.

It is to this singular location that the Banff International Literary Translation Centre invited me for a week-long stay, along with some twenty translators from around the world.

An instructive holiday indeed. From the moment of my arrival, daily exchanges took place in English, French and Spanish with Latin American, Anglo-Saxon, Bulgarian, Korean, Cree, Québécois and Norwegian accents, engendering at any given moment a truly Babelian state of chaos.

And what do translators in residency discuss? Lexicology, punctuation, Polish prosody and Castilian metrics, *Don Quichotte* and William Faulkner, more William Faulkner, semantics and intention, Galician onomastics, tone, style, philology, the surprising documentary challenges of *Moby Dick* and, in passing, the cafeteria's special of the day.

Even when fully engaged in small talk, translators stop periodically to analyze the way in which the discussion is unfolding. A translator's brain never stops working since everything in the universe is subject to translation—from an interlocutor's gestures through the dripping of the kitchen tap to the clouds' route along the mountainside and the squealing of gophers (paranoid rodents with which the campus is infested).

Mais la traduction est bien plus qu'un biais du langage, il s'agit surtout d'une passion centrifuge. Les traducteurs sont l'inverse des bibliophiles: ils s'intéressent aux ramifications invisibles du livre, à tout ce qui déborde du texte — et non simplement au papier.

Les traducteurs souffrent en somme de cette curiosité incontrôlable que l'on appelle *humanisme.*

However, translation is much more than a language expedient, it is primarily a centrifugal passion. Unlike bibliophiles, translators are interested in the invisible ramifications of a book, in everything that spills over from the text—and not just in the paper itself.

In short, translators suffer from that unbridled curiosity we call *humanism*.

Translation by S. Ouriou

Contributor Bios

Juliana Borrero (2008) is a Colombian writer, translator and researcher of language and embodiment. She has translated Edgar Allan Poe, Rudyard Kipling and Dylan Thomas, and is currently translating *Aureole* by Carole Maso, which was the purpose of her residency in Banff. She is a professor at the Universidad Pedagógica y Tecnológica in Tunja, Colombia.

Odile Cisneros (2006) received a PhD in Spanish and Portuguese from NYU and now teaches in the Department of Modern Languages and Cultural Studies and the Program in Comparative Literature at the University of Alberta in Edmonton, Canada. She co-edited *Novas: Selected Writings of Haroldo de Campos* (Evanston: Northwestern UP, 2007) and has translated the poetry of Régis Bonvicino, Haroldo de Campos, Rodrigo Rey Rosa and Jaroslav Seifert among others. At BILTC, she worked on the complete translation from Portuguese of Haroldo de Campos's *Galáxias* in collaboration with Suzanne Jill Levine.

paulo da costa (2006) was born in Angola and raised in Portugal. He is a writer, editor and translator living on the west coast of Canada.

Nicolas Dickner (2007) was born in Rivière-du-Loup, Quebec and studied fine arts and literature from 1990 to 1997. He has worked as a cultural organizer (New Brunswick, 1997), stage technician (Quebec City, 1998), exchange program employee (Dominican Republic, 1999), documentalist (Montreal, 1999) and website designer (Peru, 2000). His writing career officially began with the publication in 2000 of *L'Encyclopédie du petit cercle* but picked up speed with his first novel, *Nikolski*, published in 2005. Currently, he resides in Montreal.

Sheila Fischman (2004) is the author of more than 125 translations from French to English, principally of novels, plays and short stories by contemporary Quebec writers. She has won numerous prestigious awards for her translations and was appointed a Member of the Order of Canada in 2000 and a Chevalier of the Ordre national du Québec in 2008.

Sara Fruner (2006) received her English Literature and Language degree from Ca' Foscari University (Venice) then took two post-graduate Master's degrees in Literary Translation (English to Italian) at Ca' Foscari and ISIT (Milan). Since 2003 she has worked as a translator, proof-reader and literary talent scout for Giunti Editore and other smaller publishers.
Her interest in the post-colonial literary scene has led her to translate, among others, Canadian Poet Laureate Dionne Brand—both fiction and poetry—Monique Truong, Sello Duiker and Raj Rao.

André Gabastou (2007) translates Spanish (Carmen Laforet, Enrique Vila-Matas, Bernard Atxaga, etc.) and Latin-American writers (Adolfo Bioy Casares, Victoria Ocampo, Alan Pauls, Horacio Castellanos Moya, etc.) He teaches literary translation at the Université d'Angers and in Brussels. He is the vice-president of Atlas (Assises de la traduction littéraire à Arles/Arles Literary Translation Conference).

Patricia Godbout (2003/2005) sat on BILTC's Advisory Council from 2006 to 2008 and participated twice in the residency program as a faculty member. She is a translator and professor at the Université de Sherbrooke (Sherbrooke, Quebec) where she also heads the Centre Anne-Hébert. She has done research on translators as fictional characters in Quebec novels since 1960.

Edith Grossman (2007) is a translator, critic and occasional teacher of literature in Spanish. She was born in Philadelphia, attended the University of Pennsylvania and the University of California at Berkeley, completed a PhD at New York University, and has been the recipient of awards and honors including Fulbright, Woodrow Wilson, and Guggenheim Fellowships, the PEN Ralph Manheim Medal for Translation, an Award in Literature from the American Academy of Arts and Letters, and induction into the American Academy of Arts and Sciences. Grossman has brought over into English poetry, fiction, and non-fiction by major Latin American writers, including Gabriel García Márquez, Carlos Fuentes, Mario Vargas Llosa, Alvaro Mutis and Mayra Montero. Peninsular works that she has translated include *Don Quixote*, by Miguel de Cervantes, novels by Julián Ríos, Carmen Laforet, and Antonio Muñoz Molina, and poetry of the sixteenth and seventeenth centuries. She lives in Manhattan and has two sons, both of whom are musicians.

Raymundo Isidro Alavez (2009) is a professor in the Facultad de Estudios Superiores Acatlán (FESA) at the Universidad Nacional Autónoma de México (UNAM) and has also taught in the Political Science and Public Administration program there. He teaches Hñähñu—or Otomí, his mother tongue—in the BA program in Communications and History in the Centro de Enseñanza de Idiomas (Language Teaching Centre), and has also worked as a journalist for the newspaper *Síntesis de Hidalgo.*

Lazer Lederhendler (2007) has been translating professionally for over thirty years. He was nominated for the 2006 Governor General's Literary Award for his translation of Gaétan Soucy's *The Immaculate Conception,* which was shortlisted for the Scotiabank Giller Prize and in 2007 won the Quebec Writers' Federation award for translation. The translation of *Nikolski* by Nicolas Dickner won the Governor General's Literary Award in 2008 and the 2009 QWF translation prize. He lives in Montreal with his wife Pierrette Bouchard and their son David.

Dr. Carmen Leñero (2007), a poet, singer, writer, researcher and translator, lives in Mexico City. She has her PhD in Arts and Letters from the Universidad Nacional Autónoma de México and has also studied theatrical direction and music. She has won several literary prizes and written books of poetry, children's stories and essays. She has translated from French and English and has recorded five CDs in which she sets to music and performs pieces by a number of well-known poets.

Suzanne Jill Levine (2003/2006) is a leading translator and scholar of Latin American literature, whose publications include *The Subversive Scribe; Manuel Puig and the Spider Woman;* and hundreds of contributions to major anthologies and journals including the *New Yorker,* and numerous translations of the most original novels and experimental writing from Latin America. A professor at the University of California, her many honors include National Endowment for the Arts and NEH fellowship and research grants, the first PEN USA West Prize for Literary Translation, the PEN American Center Career Achievement award, and a Guggenheim Foundation fellowship. She is currently general editor of five volumes of the works of Borges for Penguin Classics.

Alexis Levitin (2003) has placed translations in well over 200 literary magazines, including *Partisan Review, American Poetry Review, Grand Street,* and *Kenyon Review.* His thirty books include *Soulstorm* by Clarice Lispector and *Forbidden Words* by Eugenio de Andrade (both published by New Directions). His most recent books are *Tapestry of the Sun: An Anthology of Ecuadorian Poetry* and *Brazil: A Traveler's Literary Companion.*

Anne Malena (2003) is a translator and Professor of French and Translation Studies at the University of Alberta (Edmonton). She has published French translations of two novels by Kristjana Gunnars (*La maraude* and *Degré Zéro,* Leméac 1995 and 1998) as well as poetry translation (*ellipse*) and short stories by Claudine Potvin and others.

Hélène Rioux (2003), born in Montreal, has published six novels, poetry and short stories. Short-listed five times for the Governor General's award, she received the Prix France-Québec and the Ringuet prize from l'Académie des Lettres du Québec in 2008 for *Mercredi soir au bout du monde,* the Grand Prix littéraire from the Journal de Montréal and the Prix de la Société des écrivains canadiens for *Chambre avec baignoire* in 1992. A literary translator from English and Spanish into French, she has translated some forty books by Canadian writers. In 1998, she received the QSPELL translation prize for *Self* by Yann Martel and was short-listed for the QWF in 2008 for her translation of *The Memory Artists* by Jeffrey Moore. A member of XYZ magazine's editorial board, she also writes a literary column on translation in the journal *Lettres québécoises.* Her novels have been translated into English, Spanish and Bulgarian. She has two children.

Katharina Rout (2008) translates contemporary German-language fiction into English. She was born and educated in Germany before immigrating to Canada in 1987 and teaches English and Comparative Literature at Vancouver Island University in Nanaimo, British Columbia.

Françoise Roy (2007) is a Quebec-born writer and translator. She has her Master's degree in Latin-American studies and a Translation Certificate. She has written 12 books and won the following national (Mexican) awards: Literary Translation (poetry), Victoria de las Mercedes (short story), Jaccqueline Déry-Mochon (novel), Alonso Vidal (poetry) and Ditët e Naimit (poetry). She lives in Guadalajara, Mexico.

Enrique Servín Herrera (2007/2009) is a linguist, poet and translator from Chihuahua, Mexico. He has done research on language conflict phenomena and the Mexican indigenous oral tradition. He has translated into Spanish poems from Catalan, English, French, Italian, Portuguese and other languages. He has published *El Agua y la Sombra* (Water and Shadows, poetry), *Imágenes para un Reencuentro* (Images for an Encounter, anthology of world poetry), *Ralámuli Ra'ichábo* (a method for learning the Uto-Aztecan Tarahumara language) as well as several other books as a co-author. He has received the Fuentes Mares National Award for Poetry and is currently working as a cultural promoter.

Katherine Silver (2007) is an award-winning translator of Spanish and Latin American literature. Her most recent translations include *Senselessness* and *The She-Devil in the Mirror* by Horacio Castellanos Moya, and César Aira's *The Literary Conference*. She is currently working on Daniel Sada's *Almost Never* for Graywolf Press.

Medeine Tribinevičius (2009) is a writer and translator of Lithuanian literature. Her work has been published in *The Walrus, Steppe, Room, PEN International Magazine* and the *Vilnius Review*. She is currently co-translating e.e. cummings into Lithuanian, translating the novel *Tūla* by Jurgis Kuncinas into English and working on a non-fiction book about the former Soviet region.

(BILTC year of residency shown in brackets)

Acknowledgements

Grateful acknowledgement is due to the following:

For Katherine Silver's contribution
Sampsonia Way, the online magazine of City of Asylum/Pittsburgh for permission to reprint the article that appeared in 2009

For Alexis Levitin's contribution
Review Revue for permission to reprint the article from Vol. 2, Issue 3, December, 2005

For Suzanne Jill Levine's contribution
Dalkey Archive for permission to reprint the new preface to Dalkey Archive's 2009 Edition of *The Subversive Scribe: Translating Latin American Fiction* (1991)

For Edith Grossman's contribution
HarperCollins Publishing U.S.A. for permission to reprint the translator's note to the reader that appeared in their 2003 edition of *Don Quixote*

For Lazer Lederhendler's contribution
TranscUlturAl for permission to reprint excerpts from the article published in its 2009 issue. The full article can be viewed at: http://ejournals.library.ualberta.ca/index.php/TC/article/view/6423/5416

For Nicolas Dickner's contribution
www.voir.ca for permission to reprint the article published in its July 2007 issue

Works Cited

Sarah Fruner

Brand, Dionne. *No Language is Neutral.* Toronto: McClelland & Stewart, 1998.

De Luca, Erri. "Traducendo si diventa scrittori." *Ci salverà la belleza.* I quaderni della Fiera Internazionale del Libro di Torino – Edizione 2008. Turin: Instar Libri (2009)

Raymundo Isidro Alavez

Beristaín, Helena. *Diccionario de Retórica y Poética. Editorial Porrúa.* 8th edition, 4th reprint. Mexico: Instituto de Investigaciones Filológicas de la Universidad Nacional Autónoma de México, 2003

Kintana, Dr. Garribay and Ángel María. *Historia de la Literatura Náhuatl,* tomo I. México: Editorial Porrúa, 1987 edition.

León-Portilla, Miguel. *Visión de los vencidos, Relaciones indígenas de la conquista.* Mexico: Universidad Nacional Autónoma de México. Biblioteca del estudiante universitario. Reprint of 29th edition, 2008.

Pérez Rioja, José Antonio. *Diccionario Literario.* Madrid, Spain: Editorial Tecnos,1977.

Thaayrohyadi, Serafín. *La palabra sagrada, Ro mäka Hñä. Letras indígenas contemporáneas 20.* CONACULTA - Instituto Nacional indigenista co-edition. First edition. Mexico D. F., 1998.

Wright Carr, David Charles. "Lengua, Cultura e Historia de los Otomíes." *Revista de Arqueología Mexicana: Otomíes un pueblo olvidado.* vol. XIII, Núm. 73 (mayo junio 2005) : 26-29.

Carmen Leñero

Crozier, Lorna. *La perspectiva del gato,* translated by Carmen Leñero. Mexico: Trilce Ediciones-CONACULTA, 2009.

———. *Bones in Their Wings.* Regina SK: Hagios Press, 2003.

———. *Apocrypha of Light.* Toronto: McClelland & Stewart, 2002

———. *Inventing the Hawk.* Toronto: McClelland & Stewart, 1992.

———. *Angels of Flesh, Angels of Silence.* Toronto: McClelland & Stewart, 1988.

Leñero, Carmen. "El caracol sonoro: reflexiones sobre el lenguaje de la música en relación con la poesía," colección de bolsillo No. 29, México: IIFL-UNAM, 2006.

Juliana Borrero

Brossard, Nicole. "Kind skin my mind," translated by Marlene Wildeman. *Trivia: A journal of ideas*, No. 12 (1988).

Causse, Michelle and Lise Weil. "Conversation with Michelle Causse." Trivia: Voices of feminism, Issue 3 at http://triviavoices.net/archives/issue3/index.html.

Gould, Karen. *Writing in the feminine: feminism and experimental writing in Quebec.* Carbondale and Edwardsville: Southern Illinois University Press, 1990.

Maso, Carole. "Except Joy: on *Aureole*," in Maso, *Break every rule: Essays on language, longing, moments of desire.* Washington DC: Counterpoint, 2000.

———. *Aureole.* New Jersey: The Ecco Press,1996.

Mallet, Brian. Unpublished notes from a conference. Bogota: Universidad de los Andes, 1998.

Scott, Gail. *Spaces like Stairs.* Toronto: The Women's Press, 1989.

Spivak, Gayatri. "The Politics of Translation," in Lawrence Venuti (ed.), *The Translation Studies Reader.* London and New York: Routledge, 2000.

Von Flotow, Luise. *Translation and gender: Translating in the 'era of feminism.'* Shanghai: Shanghai Foreign Language Education Press, 2007.

Warland, Betsy. "the breasts refuse." *Trivia: A journal of ideas*, Issue 13 (Fall 1988)

Odile Cisneros

Campos, Haroldo de. *Galáxias.* 2nd ed. São Paulo: Editora 34, 2004.

———. "Translation as Creation and Criticism," in Sérgio Bessa and Odile Cisneros (eds.), *Novas: Selected Writings.* Evanston: Northwestern University Press, 2007.

Jackson, K. David. "Traveling in Haroldo de Campos's *Galáxias*: A Guide and Notes for the Reader." *Ciberletras* 17 (2007).

Pound, Ezra. *Translations.* New York: New Directions, 1963.

Weinberger, Eliot. "Anonymous Sources," in Daniel Balderston and Marcy E. Schwartz (eds.), *Voice-Overs: Translation and Latin American Literature.* Albany: State University of New York Press, 2002.

Anne Malena

Barthes, Roland. *Sade, Fourier, Loyola.* Paris: Éditions du Seuil, 1971.

Cossman, Brenda, Shannon Bell, Lise Gotell and Becki L. Ross. *Bad Attitude/s on Trial: Pornography, Feminism, and the Butler Decision.* Toronto: University of Toronto Press, 1997.

"Erotic." *Oxford English Dictionary Online.* May 15, 2007.

———. *Webster's New World Dictionary.* 3rd edition. 1988.

Grosz, Elizabeth. "The Time of Violence; Deconstruction and Value." *College Literature* 26.1 (1999): 8–18.

Kappeler, Susanne. *The Pornography of Representation.* Minneapolis: University of Minnesota Press, 1986.

Kostash, Myrna. "Flesh and the Devil: Eroticism and the Body Politic," in Sylvie Gilbert (ed.), *Arousing Sensation: A Case Study of Controversy Surrounding Art and the Erotic.* Banff, AB: Banff Centre Press,1999.

"Pornography". *Oxford English Dictionary Online.* May 15, 2007.

———. *Webster's New World Dictionary.* 3rd edition. 1988.

Potvin, Claudine. "Écrire ma 'dominatrix.'" Unpublished manuscript.

———. *Pornographies.* Quebec City: L'Instant même, 1993.

Sontag, Susan. *Styles of Radical Will.* New York: Picador, 2002.

Patricia Godbout

Derrida, Jacques. "What Is a 'Relevant Translation'?" translated by Lawrence Venuti. Critical Inquiry, 27 (2001): 174–200.

——— . *Qu'est-ce qu'une traduction « relevante »?*, Paris : Éditions de l'Herne, 2005 [1999].

Douglass, Frederick. 2006. *La vie de Frederick Douglass, esclave américain, écrite par lui-même,* trans. by Hélène Tronc, Paris, Gallimard, coll. « La Bibliothèque Gallimard » (no 182).

Du Bois, W. E. B. *Les âmes du peuple noir,* translated by Magali Bessone. Paris: La Découverte / Poche, 2007.

Ellison, Ralph. 2003. *Homme invisible, pour qui chantes-tu?,* trans. by Magali et Robert Merle, Paris, Grasset.

Gilroy, Paul. 2003. *L'Atlantique noir. Modernité et double conscience*, trans. by Jean-Philippe Henkel, Paris, Kargo.

Hurston, Zora Neale. 2006. *Des pas dans la poussière*, trans. by Françoise Brodsky, La Tour d'Aigues (France), L'Aube.

Hegel, Georg Wilhelm Friedrich. *Phénoménologie de l'Esprit*, translated by Jean Hyppolite. Paris : Aubier-Montaigne, 1946.

———. *Phénoménologie de l'Esprit*, translated by Jean-Pierre Lefebvre. Paris: Aubier, 1991.

Siemerling, Winfried. *The New North American Studies. Culture, writing, and the politics of re/cognition*, London and New York: Routledge, 2005.

———. *Récits nord-américains d'émergence : culture, écriture et politique de re/connaissance*, translated by Patricia Godbout. Quebec: Presses de l'Université Laval, 2010.

Washington, Booker T. 2008. *Up from Slavery. Autobiographie d'un esclave émancipé*, trans. by Jeanne-Marie Vazelle, Paris, Les Éditeurs libres.

Lazer Lederhendler

Biron, Michel, François Dumont, Elisabeth Nardout-Lafarge. *Histoire de la littérature québécoise*. Montreal: Boréal, 2007.

Camus, Albert. *L'Étranger*. Paris: Gallimard, 1942.

Cardinal, Pierre. "Regard critique sur la traduction au Canada." *Meta*, vol. 23, no. 2 (1978): 141–47. http://id.erudit.org/iderudit/002204ar

Dickner, Nicolas. *Nikolski*. Quebec: Alto, 2005.

———. *Nikolski*, translated by Lazer Lederhendler. Toronto: Knopf Canada, 2008.

Driver, Harold E. *Indians of North America, Second Edition, Revised*. Chicago: The University of Chicago Press, 1969.

Eaglestone, Robert. "Levinas, Translation, and Ethics," in Sandra Bermann and Michael Wood (eds.), *Nation, Language, and the Ethics of Translation*. Princeton, NJ: Princeton University Press, 2005. (127–38.)

FLQ. "Manifeste du Front de Libération du Québec." October 1970. http://pages infinit.net/histoire/manifst_flq.html

Grant, Pamela, and Kathy Mezei. "Background to Literary Translation in Canada." 28 Aug. 2008. http://compcanlit.usherbrooke.ca/about_translation.html

Jakobson, Roman. "On Linguistic Aspects of Translation," in Jakobson, *Language in Literature*. Cambridge, MA: Belknap-Harvard University Press,1987.

Lamb, W. Kaye. "Canada." 25 Sept. 2008.
http://www.thecanadianencyclopedia.com

Paz, Octavio. "Translation: Literature and Letters, " in Rainer Schulte and John Biguenet (eds.), *Theories of Translation: An Anthology of Essays from Dryden to Derrida*. Chicago: The University of Chicago Press, 1992. (152–62.)

Simon, Sherry. *Translating Montreal: Episodes in the Life of a Divided City*. Montreal: McGill-Queen's University Press, 2006.

The Truman Show. Dir. Peter Weir. Perf. Jim Carrey, Laura Linney. Paramount Pictures, 1998.

Vallières, Pierre. *Nègres blancs d'Amérique*. Montreal: Parti pris, 1968.

Venuti, Lawrence. *The Scandals of Translation: Towards an Ethics of Difference*. London: Routledge, 1998.

Weinberger, Eliot. "Anonymous Sources: A Talk on Translators & Translation." Fascicle Issue 01 (Summer 2005). http://www.fascicle.com/issue01/Poets/weinberger1.htm

Susan Ouriou is a Governor General's award-winning translator and fiction writer. She has translated over twenty novels by Quebec, Spanish and Mexican authors and has written a novel, *Damselfish*, and numerous short stories. She is currently the director of the Banff International Literary Translation Centre.